"*Dan Montgomery affirms the meanings of love as . . . voluntary vulnerability . . . the willingness to risk being ourselves . . . deepening trust . . . the freedom to grow . . . truly valuing another. COURAGE TO LOVE is a helpful book for the person working through feelings of rejection, betrayal, loneliness or bitterness from the pain of life's frequent tragedies.*"

—David Augsburger

"*. . . a practical manual on the art of loving. The author has the unique ability—and knowledge—to deal with psychological principles from a Christian perspective. I commend it to everyone who wants to know how to love.*"

—Dr. Alan Loy McGinnis

courage to love

by dan montgomery

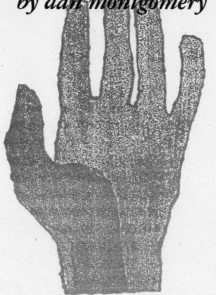

GL Regal Books A Division of G/L Publications
Glendale, California, U.S.A.

Other Good Regal reading:
Caring Enough to Confront by David Augsburger
Can You Love Yourself? by Jo Berry
Do I Have to Be Me? by Lloyd H. Ahlem
How to Cope by Lloyd H. Ahlem
Your Churning Place by Robert Wise

The foreign language publishing of all Regal books is under the direction of GLINT. GLINT provides financial and technical help for the adaptation, translation and publishing of books in more than 85 languages for millions of people worldwide.

For more information write: GLINT, 110 W. Broadway, Glendale, California 91204

Scripture quotations, unless otherwise indicated, are from the *New American Standard Bible*.© The Lockman Foundation 1960, 1962, 1963, 1968, 1971. Used by permission.
Other versions include:
TLB From *The Living Bible,* Copyright ©1971 by Tyndale House Publishers, Wheaton, Illinois. Used by permission.
NIV The New International Version, Holy Bible. Copyright ©1978 by New York International Bible Society. Used by permission.
KJV Authorized King James Version

Published by Regal Books Division, G/L Publications
Glendale, California 91209
Printed in U.S.A.

Library of Congress Catalog Card No. 79-65421
ISBN 0-8307-0720-4

Case histories used in this book are true. Names have been changed to protect the confidence of those who experienced them.

...to Tammie

Contents

Foreword

Dan Montgomery has written a book we all need very much.

Despite the tremendous interest in *koinonia*, body life, small groups and interpersonal relationships over the past 10 to 15 years, many Christians still feel isolated, alone, and unloved

There seems to be something in us (could it be what Paul describes so graphically in Romans 3?) that keeps us from reaching out to one another easily and naturally in genuine Christian love. A few of us do it well. A few more make efforts ranging from heroic to half-hearted. But a great part of the Body of Christ still lies in the grip of apathy, suspicion and fear.

We just don't seem to trust one another—at least not easily. And many of us feel we can justify our distrust. We all have our personal tales of how we have been psychologically ripped off, rejected or just plain cut up in little pieces, and all too often by Christian friends or members of our own church.

The apostle John tells us that perfect love casts out fear, but as Dan points out, we are all afraid. We are all in the same boat when it comes to fear. All too often, fear casts out love and the Body suffers because its members suffer.

In addition to counseling others who are hurting, Dan has experienced his own share of suffering—of being betrayed and rejected. He has grappled personally with the question he presents early in chapter 1:

> What do you do when you feel that you are walking within the will of God, and suddenly the direction of life takes a turn that you neither understand nor accept?

Finding the answer to that question is what this book is all about. Dan doesn't claim to have all the pieces to the puzzle, but he is pointing in the right direction as he follows after Jesus Christ.

Dan has found new courage to love, and he wants to help others find it as well so that all the world will know that we are His disciples, as we have love one for another.

Fritz Ridenour

For the friendship, insight, and prayer shared throughout the book's development, I wish to express my heartfelt thanks to Karin Presley, Florence Blakeley, Norm and Kaaren Juggert, Keith Ewing, Shirley Felt, Vince Gil, Cindi Gamez, Jan Root, Fritz Ridenour and Everett Shostrom.

Introduction

A blaze of emotion has carried the message burning in my heart onto these pages. We all have wrestled with shattered hopes, betrayed commitments, and loss of dignity. I have longed to do something about this suffering.

How can we find our way through the valley of pain? How can we come out the other side brimming with life and hope? How can we, after being hurt so deeply, find the courage to love?

As a Christian psychologist I devote myself to healing and growth. I do many of the same things my colleagues do who would not consider themselves to be Christians. I draw upon theory and techniques from diverse schools of psychological thought such as psychodrama, psychoanalysis, behavior modification, bioenergetics, and existential psychotherapy. However, I integrate these psychological resources with an active trust in the Holy Spirit.

My focus in counseling is the whole person: body, feelings, and spirit. The body speaks its own language; it always tells the truth about our experiences in life. I often work directly with the body because it is a trustworthy instrument of wisdom and intuition.

I listen carefully to the innermost feelings of those who entrust themselves to my care. We can always recognize a feeling because it is the hardest thing to tell someone. A feeling is the private, emotionally colored way that we experience life. Expressing our feelings makes us vulnerable to criticism or rejection by others. But not expressing them confines us to a dungeon of our own making where we hide our real selves from the world and from God. If we stay hidden in the dungeon for too long, we lose all sense of who we are and what our mission in life is.

The spiritual dimension of counseling involves looking for how God can minister life, love, and courage when we are in the valley of pain and suffering. The God of the Christian faith is Lord of both the mountaintops and the valleys. Often our sufferings and betrayals lead to deeper trust in Him. In surrendering to our inner pain we can find Jesus, the wisest of all counselors. He embraces us in the solitude of our suffering because He, too, knows what it feels like to be bruised, wounded, and humiliated. But He also knows the secret of being raised from the bed of suffering so that the last word is one of triumph, joy, and peace.

So in my work as a counselor I combine the tools of modern therapeutic psychology with a faith that God will bring wholeness and direction to people's lives. My friends whose sufferings prompted me to write this book are each finding their way. If you suffer with wounds from life, you can find your way too.

God desires you to experience much more of your total self than you have yet realized. He wants to transform your *whole* personality, including the parts you find "unacceptable." Painful feelings of betrayal, rejection, guilt, confusion, and depression are not to be avoided. They are to be surrendered to and worked with, as clay in a potter's hands. This is the secret of having our lives shaped by the hand of God.

I invite you to come on a journey of self-exploration. Find out how your fears, hurts, and rejections can be faced and changed into the courage to love.

1
Loving Makes You Vulnerable

Pain is no evil unless it conquers us—George Eliot

I lay still on the bed in my tiny dormitory. My heart ached. My breathing was heavy—*so* heavy, like someone had dropped a load of bricks on my chest. I was sobbing so deeply that it frightened me. It lasted for two hours, then subsided and I knew I had made it through another day.

It took me weeks to get over the intense pain and months to recollect myself completely after Beth and I broke up. I loved her so much. And she loved me. I believed that my prayers for a wife and life-companion had been answered in our relationship. I had prayed steadily for four years, ever since my conversion to the Lord in my early twenties.

Hadn't the Lord guided and blessed our relationship? We had much fruit to show for it: peace, trust, honesty, and love. But then it suddenly ended. Beth called and said we would never see each other again. She said she had sincerely thought that we would be married, but then in our two-week school break over Christmas she decided to go back to a relationship with her former boyfriend. Eventually they were married. And I was once again left alone...with God.

A Rose by Any Other Name

Most of us in our Christian walks have experienced the pain and confusion that comes with feeling betrayed and rejected. *But what do you do when you feel that you are walking within the will of God, and suddenly life takes a turn that you can neither understand nor accept?* One of the biggest challenges of the Christian life is to transform the hurts, pains, and frustrations that we all experience into a *growth process* that contributes to our maturity in the Lord.

Paul expresses this principle in Romans 8:28: "And we know that *all* things work together for good to them that love God, to them who are the called according to his purpose" *(KJV,* italics added).

An African Christian, who had suffered the loss of his family in the massacre of Leopoldville, once told me that a Christian is like a rose. God allows the bad and painful experiences of life to act as fertilizer. In so doing, He neutralizes the poisonous effects of pain, and actually makes it serve His purposes by transforming it into the blessedness of His will.

Often as Christians we believe that the sooner we get rid of our pain and put on a smiling, victorious face, the sooner we will get back on the track of God's will. However, this approach tends to do the exact opposite. For in our desire to *act* as though we feel fine or as though we have great faith, we in fact must repress or hide our deep inner feelings of pain. In so doing, we lose touch with ourselves, and we also lose our sensitivity to what God is trying to teach us through the process of genuine suffering.

The task of the rose is not to pretend that the fertilizer is not there, or to get rid of the fertilizer by absorbing it all at once. Rather, when fertilizer has been administered to the rose by a helpful gardener, the rose must simply be patient enough to allow some days and even weeks to pass while the fertilizer is drawn up through the roots into the rose's life and gradually assimilated.

The fertilizer is profoundly changed. It loses its nature as poisonous and foul-smelling waste. It becomes the rose itself. The dung becomes the delicate and fragrant blooms of the growing plant.

It seems to me that this was happening to Beth and me as through God's providence we were called to part ways. We both felt great pain and confusion. But we both had faith that God was somehow moving us along the best possible pathways for our lives.

The important point here is that I had faith that God was still guiding my life, but I *felt* hurt, lonely, and confused about how He was doing it. So for several months I was called to creatively bear the burden of emotional and psychological pain, while also having faith that God was at work in my life "to will and to work for His good pleasure" (Phil. 2:13).

I prayed often about how to handle the pain. The Lord showed me to own up to it honestly and to express it whenever it reached the point of causing me to cry. So I went about the normal business and responsibilities of life and, when the urge came, I would draw aside from people and spend some time quietly crying and releasing the hurt feelings.

Jesus Knows About Pain, Too

It took time and patience for the deep inner wound to begin to mend. And this is how it is for all of us. The loss may have been the death of a loved one, the change of employment, a misunderstanding in a friendship, or the shattering of a dream, but what remains the same is the very human experience of hurt and pain. Jesus also experienced and expressed these feelings. Although He was filled with the Holy Spirit without measure, on many occasions He was hurt by misunderstandings from close friends or by the very mission that God had appointed to Him. The Scriptures say of Jesus that "although He was a Son, He learned obedience from the things which He suffered" (Heb. 5:8).

This is vital to our understanding of Jesus because He is the heart and soul of the Christian life. It is by surrendering to His presence in our lives as the risen Christ and author of our salvation (see Heb. 2:10) that we become more and more like Him.

Jesus Helps Us Be Human

To grow in Christlikeness, we experience more fully *both* our human and divine nature. To see some of the very real ways that Jesus suffered psychological and emotional pain, consider the following Scriptures *(KJV)*. In Matthew 26:38 He was "exceedingly sorrowful"; in John 11:33 He "groaned in the spirit"; in Mark 3:5 He was "grieved"; in John 12:27 He was "troubled"; in John 11:35 He "wept"; and in Hebrews 5:7 He prayed with "strong crying and tears."

Jesus experienced His humanness fully, as we can learn to do. Yet the anchor of His life was His abiding and unshakable union with the Father in His innermost being. So He could feel disappointment, frustration, hurt, or pain and express these feelings openly, while also trusting the Father's will to be done no matter how much inner pain He experienced.

The greatest example of Jesus' suffering is when He knelt in the garden of Gethsemane and prayed that, if it was possible, the Father might spare Him the ordeal of humiliation, betrayal and death that was about to happen. So intense was the emotional pain that He fell down on the ground (see Mark 14:35) and prayed in great agony (see Luke 22:44). The other side of Jesus' agony was the joy He anticipated in doing the Father's will. In Hebrews 12:2 we are encouraged to fix "our eyes on Jesus the author and perfecter of faith, who for the joy set before Him endured the cross.'' Jesus had great faith, but He *felt* very much alone in the world as He surrendered with His whole being to the mission God had chosen for Him.

What Jesus so wonderfully teaches us is that God's yes to our lives—His mission for us that He has chosen from the foundations of the earth—is greater than any negative experiences we have along the journey of life. With Jesus' help, and the support of the Holy Spirit who dwells in our innermost being, we too can say *Yes!* to life, while experiencing both the positive and negative psychological dimensions of our humanness.

Theologian Morton Kelsey writes:

Really meeting the God who is love means stepping willingly into the refining fire to be slowly remade and changed....For some inscrutable reason, something hidden deep in His nature, He wants to meet the totality of us, good, bad, and indifferent, in the greatest depth. And only then can His love touch every part of us and transform or change the whole.[1]

So it happened with Beth and me. After a period of several weeks of feeling stunned with pain, a flow of healing love began to well up little by little from deep within. I began to pray for God's best for her even though I knew I would never see her again. I began to surrender to Him my broken heart so that He could remake and change it in ways that He desired.

And it wasn't long before I recognized that still, small voice within: ''Dan, you have learned much about life from this relationship. Having known the joy of love and friendship, and having now experienced the pain of following my path for you, are you willing to love again?'' the Lord asked. And my answer surprised even me. With all the energy of my being I shouted: "Yes! Yes, Lord, I am willing—because it was precious. It was real. We were both changed because of the love we shared and the trust we had in you!"

I Lost My Fear of Loving

And this experience became a turning point in my life. By the grace of God I began to lose my fear of loving. Knowing that I could make it through the pain, and realizing that pain is sometimes a vital part of growth, I felt a new courage to open my life to other people and to risk the joy and the pain of heartfelt love. I decided to withdraw my demand of a guarantee that I never be hurt or disappointed. I decided to no longer demand that everything always work out perfectly without any pain, frustration, or confusion. I decided to own more fully my humanness, yet trust God more fully to be at work in my life.

These commitments have had a great impact on my life. I believe that through the crucible of suffering I discovered an essential fact of spiritual growth. We grow most when we relax and surrender to what God is allowing to happen to us in the normal flow of our lives. Not that we become passive. We actively trust God to wisely intervene in every miraculous way that He chooses, and we expect His blessings to guide us through life, but we give up our demand that life will always be pleasant or easy.

We accept that God works as effectively through adversity, hardship, and pain as He does through blessing, comfort, and miraculous intervention. In this *growth process* we learn to know Jesus intimately in both the "fellowship of His sufferings" and the "power of His resurrection" (Phil. 3:10).

I am now married to my precious wife and friend, Tammie. Looking back I see the wisdom of the Lord as I never could have imagined it then. He *is* faithful! I mean unbelievably, miraculously faithful—to fulfill our heart's desires far beyond what we could imagine or even hope for. All things *do* work together for those who love God and seek to find His purpose in their lives. And now as I gaze at the woman God gave me as the life companion I so deeply longed for, I am genuinely moved by His love and wisdom. We are building, with His help, a relationship that allows for the flow of much love and support, yet encourages us each to keep discovering the unique missions that God has called us to fulfill. And I am increasingly free to flow with love toward God and toward other people.

In this book I want to help you learn to deal with the pain, anxiety, and fear that we all feel from time to time. As we will see in the next chapter, the flow of love in our lives is analogous to the flow of water through the inner core of a well. Negative emotional experiences, like debris in a well, can block the flow of love. What we want to do is learn how to keep our inner cores clean so that we can be continually filled with the love that God supplies.

By learning to face and handle the pains and fears that life inevitably brings our way, we can lose our fear of loving and gain the courage to love again—and again.

Workshop

1. Have you ever had an experience like the author's in which you thought you were walking in the will of God and suddenly life took a turn that you could not understand or accept?

Have you come to terms with that experience or does it still bother you?

2. Can you identify with the author's illustration of the rose and the fertilizer?

What experience are you having right now, or what experience have you had recently that you could describe as ''fertilizer'' for your Christian growth?

3. Reread the section in which the author describes the psychological and emotional pain suffered by Jesus. Do these descriptions fit your image of Christ? Why or why not?

Does Jesus' susceptibility to pain and frustration make Him seem weak to you? Why or why not?

4. Reread Morton Kelsey's statement which begins: "Really meeting the God who is love means stepping willingly into the refining fire to be slowly remade and changed." Would you say you are doing this? In what way?

2
Growing in Dignity, Courage and Love

We are empty vessels to be filled by the Lord. To be filled with the life of Jesus in accordance with who we deeply are is the Christian definition of self-fulfillment—Adrian Van Kaam

When Jesus encountered the Samaritan woman at the site of Jacob's well, He gave her an illustration that still speaks to us in the twentieth century.

He told her that she herself was like the well, and that He was a source of "living water" that could well up within her so as to quench her thirst for meaning in life.

Jesus said to her: "Whoever drinks of the water that I shall give him shall never thirst; but the water that I shall give him shall become in him a well of water springing up to eternal life" (John 4:14).

Think about it. In addressing this woman Jesus spoke intimately to us. He taught that we each are like a well, and that God's gift to us is an unending supply of spiritual water that will cause us to be refreshed and to find meaning in life.

A well has a center or core through which water from a source outside the well flows into and then through the well. In like manner people have a core or spiritual center through which the very life of God can flow.

In surrendering our life to Jesus we, like the Samaritan woman, make Him the dynamic spiritual source of our lives. When we surrender to Him, we activate the inner well and, from then on, the spiritual water that Jesus gives wells up within us with a daily supply of wisdom and inner direction for how we are to live our lives.

The spiritual core of our being reflects that we are created in the image of God, and that we share with God the capacities for awareness, choice, and intimacy. The very uniqueness of Christianity is the proclamation that through Christ you can have the presence of God abide within your innermost being. And, having God dwell within, you can have a steady source of guidance through the journey of life. King Solomon understood this well when he wrote: "For wisdom and truth will enter the very center of your being, filling your life with joy" (Prov. 2:10, *TLB*).

What Spiritual Water Really Means

The living water or spiritual water that Jesus promised us can be understood in terms of three vital qualities that flow from our inner wells. The qualities are *dignity, courage,* and *love*.

A powerful example of how these qualities flowed freely in the life of Jesus is stated in Philippians 2:6-8. Paul writes of Jesus that "although He existed in the form of God," He "did not regard equality with God a thing to be grasped, but emptied Himself, taking the form of a bondservant, and being made in the likeness of men." And, further, Jesus "humbled Himself by becoming obedient to the point of death, even death on a cross." Although Jesus had the very *dignity* of God, He had such pure *love* for people that He *courageously* gave up His own earthly life so that humanity—you and me—could have the right and the power to become God's own children (see John 1:12).

This passage from Philippians reveals God's plan of

salvation but it also shows the nature of Christ. Paul prefaces these words by appealing to us to have the same attitudes that Christ had (see Phil. 2:5).

It could be a bit overwhelming if we thought that we were supposed to be perfect, like Jesus. But the Bible also teaches that the Kingdom of God is like a mustard seed (see Matt. 13:31) in that personal growth is more slow and steady than it is sudden and dramatic.

Therefore, we can have real hope for growth in the qualities of dignity, courage, and love throughout our lifetimes. The growth may be slow, but it is persistent!

The Meanings of Dignity, Courage, and Love

Dignity is the sense of being worthy or honorable. Reduced to its simplest level, it is the inner affirmation that your life has great value. This is the good news or gospel that Jesus came into the world to proclaim. Our lives are precious. What Jesus is by nature, we have become by the grace of God— sons and daughters of the living God. Theologian Adrian Van Kaam writes:

> We will see in eternal gratefulness how the inner spring of grace made our deepest self similar to Jesus. We will see how the spring inside us leaps up with dazzling splendor for all eternity.[2]

For the Christian, the fact that by grace he or she is the glory of Christ (see John 17:22) gives life very special meaning. Knowing how deeply God loves us, we can have courage to surrender to His unfolding will just as Jesus did. That surrender allows God's own dignity to flow through us daily, cleansing our lives of superficial sources, and enabling us to become the courageous and loving persons He calls us to be.

Courage is the quality that lets us take a stand in life for values that we believe in. As the Scriptures say, we are to be "doers of the word, and not hearers only" (Jas. 1:22, *KJV*).

We do not have to think only in terms of dramatic acts of bravery. There is a more hidden side of courage that has to do with the way we live each day in the most ordinary circumstances. For instance, do we express our feelings, thoughts, and values—even in the face of disagreement or belittlement—in open and direct ways? Jesus did, and His presence in the core of our lives gently urges us to radiate our inner values in daily life.

Courage enables us to recognize and face squarely the difficult, painful, or dangerous aspects of life. With courage we can assert ourselves in ways that the Spirit prompts us to seek truth, love, and justice in the world. And we can draw great comfort from knowing that the same Spirit that inspires us to be courageous is the Spirit whom Jesus called the Comforter and Helper.

Love involves feeling emotionally and spiritually connected to others. Love is the lifeblood of the Christian life. Jesus said: "By this all men will know that you are My disciples, if you have love for one another" (John 13:35).

But love is more than a feeling; it is a commitment, in the face of pain or sacrifice, to the highest good of another person. This is how God relates to humanity and how He inspires us to relate to one another. Love brings a sense of excitement and freshness to life. We feel like we belong with others, and that we can creatively express our feelings, values, gifts, talents, and energies. Love brings respect for individual differences. It frees people to have confidence in their own originality and to deeply appreciate the uniqueness of others. Outgoing deeds of concrete service flow from our lives when we are being channels for the Living Water.

Sister Maria Is a Channel of Living Water

A beautiful illustration of how all this works in the life of the maturing Christian comes to mind as I recall a conversation I had with a Catholic nun.

It was Christmas and I had been having a wonderful time with my family. We had shared good food and fellowship for several days.

The day after Christmas I met Sister Maria downtown. I asked how her Christmas had been. She said, ''Oh, Dan. I had the most marvelous Christmas! At the school where I work there is a little girl who several months ago had contracted cancer of the bone in her leg. The doctors said she would only live a couple more years. In surgery they amputated her leg. Only several weeks before all this happened the little girl's family had started attending a prayer and Bible study fellowship in our parish. The wonderful thing was to see how they all surrounded the little girl with love. And she took it so well. She was a great example of courage to all of us. Anyway, that family invited me to spend Christmas with them. Even though there is much suffering in the family, we still had the most precious and loving Christmas I have ever had!''

This conversation stirred me deeply. How remarkably did the dignity, courage, and love of Jesus show through the lives of both Sister Maria and the little girl! Such a strong, reliable flow of God's grace through Sister Maria's life is the result of several decades of an abiding walk with Christ. She has opened up the depths of her being to the flow of God's love, and now most anyone who spends time with her feels that in knowing Maria they know something of Jesus.

But Maria has also known suffering, pain, and failure in her spiritual development. In other conversations she has shared with me the many times that God has had to be very patient in showing her her imperfections, prejudices, and failures—only to inspire her once again to follow Him with all her heart.

What I like most about Maria is that she is so human! Knowing her gives me courage that I too can grow over my lifetime to intimately experience and express the inner work of love that Jesus is doing in my life. Yet, in the growth process, I can also be honest about my shortcomings. I can look objectively for the debris that blocks my inner well from flowing freely. And, with God's continued grace, I can make a little more progress in removing the debris so that I become a more open channel of His living water.

What Can Block the Well Within?

In the next two chapters I will focus on two clogging factors—betrayal and fear—that can plug up the core of our inner wells. But first let me ask you a question.

How do *you* remain loving in what is often an unloving world? Do you feel that some persons or events have "done you dirt" in life? If so, what happened to you, and what are you doing to work through it?

When we have been hurt—and all of us have—there is a deeply human tendency to protect ourselves so as to never feel pain again. The problem is that we may try to relieve the hurt and overcome the emotional pain in wrong ways—ways that render us incapable of opening up to life and loving others once again. So now we turn to the subjects of how to face pain and fear, and how to keep our hearts open to love.

Workshop

1. The author states that as we express the core attributes of dignity, courage, and love in our lives we become most human and most Christlike. Do you agree or disagree? Why?

2. Of the three core attributes, which is the most important to you right now: dignity, courage or love? Why?

3. Reread Sister Maria's story. What helped the family she described to have the best Christmas of all? How can the typical Christian family experience the same type of feelings at Christmas?

3
The Pain of Betrayal

As they were eating, [Jesus] said, "Truly I say unto you that one of you will betray Me"—Matthew 26:21

Jesus is both the Saviour of the world and the greatest psychologist who ever lived. He saw—and still sees—deeply into the human heart. His loving gaze bared the souls and revealed the most intimate secrets of those who knew Him. He changed their hearts, and He changes us today.

It is this same Jesus whom we encounter in the depths of our soul. He knows the secret of our identity and our destiny. He is the pathway to our fulfillment. He administers the healing balm of divine love that gives us courage to love again, even though we have felt betrayed, bruised, and brokenhearted. Jesus also experienced these things (see Isa. 53:3-5).

We have all felt betrayed. Some of us have been betrayed many times; others only a few times. What we share with each other and with Jesus is the pain of betrayal. It is like having an axe laid to the tender roots of our being.

Betrayal by Rape

Let's look for a moment at Mary, for whom the betrayal was devastating. Yet, no one would have ever known because she hid it so perfectly for seven years. By reliving Mary's experience of betrayal with her, we can develop a deeper appreciation for the hurt and suffering everyone around us experiences. We can also develop a better understanding of the particular form our own betrayals and rejections take—and how we can gain the courage to love again.

Webster's dictionary defines betrayal in the following ways: "to break faith with; to deceive; to lead astray; to seduce and then abandon; or to fail to meet the hopes of." In the story of Mary we will find all of these principles at work.

Kelly and Mary began college together. It seemed only natural that they should date each other. He was the strong, agile athlete—handsome and popular. She was charming, witty, and petite. They were both Christians and often attended church together. Everyone said they were the perfect couple. Naturally, after a year of dating, they began to talk over the possibility of marriage.

One afternoon Kelly came to her apartment. He sat with her on the couch for awhile and then said, "Take off your clothes."

"What?" she asked.

"I mean it. We've been going together for a year now and it's time to make love. You'll like it. Now get undressed!"

Mary was stunned, and confused. It seemed as though someone had hit her inner dignity with a sledgehammer. She felt love for Kelly—at least she thought she did. While the relationship was lacking in a lot of ways, it was the closest thing she had ever known to emotional warmth with another person. She realized that everything in the relationship had always centered around Kelly, but wasn't that the way it was supposed to be?

As a pastor's daughter she had been taught to always

respect the power and authority of a man. It was a woman's place to submit—wasn't it?

Kelly got more aggressive, fondling her through her clothes. She felt a mild panic, but believed that if she just kept resisting he would stop. At least he should stop—if he respected her—shouldn't he?

As Kelly got more and more forceful, she began to feel terror. "How can this be right?" she thought. But having never talked to her parents about sex, and not having dated very much before, she simply didn't know.

When Kelly ripped off her blouse and pulled her skirt up to her waist, terror burst like a bombshell into her consciousness. He weighed 180 pounds and was very muscular. She was a slight 100 pounds. She was crying, shaking with fear, and moaning "No—No—" In the dim background she heard him laughing loudly and repeating, "You're really gonna like this."

As he penetrated her, the shame was overwhelming, as thick as a fog and as putrid as an open sewer. What happened to her dreams of love, gentleness, respect, and joy?

Shaken to the depths of her being, she felt numb and petrified by fear—and disgust. He finally reached a climax, feverishly enjoying his sexual release. She felt like a mummy in some deep dark pyramid of Egypt a thousand miles away. "It's funny," she remembered thinking, "how numb I feel. I'm not even here. He's doing something to my body, but I'm not really here. I don't feel anything anymore."

Somewhere in the haze of it all he got off of her and dressed. She lay there, eyes glazed, unmoving. He combed his hair and straightened his clothes. He looked at her and whispered, "Sorry if it hurt. I'll see you tomorrow." Then he left.

The Meaning of Betrayal

Kelly's abuse of Mary—supposedly the love of his

life—illustrates the nature of betrayal in a most heartrending way.

Betrayal is something we have all experienced in one form or another. The cast of characters in the role of villain or persecutor are innumerable: parents, brothers or sisters, uncles or aunts, neighborhood kids, schoolmates, teachers, pastors or priests, coaches, spouses, clerks, salesmen, lawyers, administrators, counselors, and even friends!

The essence of betrayal is being stripped of our dignity and used to serve someone else's purposes. This is the meaning of exploitation, manipulation, or humiliation. The result is a loss of faith on our part in a loving and nurturing world, and the development of radical defense mechanisms that seemingly ensure we will never be hurt or taken advantage of again.

Pause for a moment to recall the times in your life when you experienced the pain of betrayal. It is important for you to be aware of those memories, to bring them into the open air of consciousness. Because only then can you discover the damaging effects they may have had on your personality. With awareness you can discover how to undo the bad effects and get new growth going in your life. Mary was courageous enough to finally do this, after seven years of keeping the painful feelings buried.

What did Mary lose in the manipulative enounter with Kelly? She lost for the next seven years the most vital qualities of human life: dignity, courage, and love. The core qualities were ousted from the depths of her being, and a new set of traits came to reside there: *shame* replaced dignity; *terror* replaced courage; and *rage* replaced love.

It is my belief that all people long for fulfillment in the areas of dignity, courage, and love. But most of us are deeply frustrated in one or more of them. This frustration usually occurs when we are humiliated instead of affirmed, intimidated instead of encouraged, or exploited instead of loved. Thus, we come to have embarrassment, fear, and resentment in our core instead of dignity, courage and love.

WE WANT	WE GET	WE FEEL	WE BECOME
Dignity	Humiliation	Ashamed	Defensive
Courage	Intimidation	Fearful	Manipulative
Love	Exploitation	Resentful	Distant

Mary now had a deep, abiding sense of *inner pain*. But in order to cope with this intense pain, Mary pushed it out of awareness and numbed herself to all feeling. So the shame, terror, and rage became buried for years in the dark recesses of her unconscious.

All of us, to some degree, feel core pain. *Core pain* may be defined as the reaction of a person to the violent loss of his or her basic human dignity and his or her right to fulfillment of an original destiny inspired by God.

At the deepest level of the core, there is an expressed hurt or pain that reflects the experience: "Why am I not loved, given freedom to be myself, and appreciated for the original person that I am?"

The experience of betrayal and inner pain is universal. We are each touched by the specific form it takes in our own lives. If life has been basically nurturing for us, with only a few poisonous encounters, then we will not feel the shame, terror, and rage that Mary felt. Our experience of inner pain will be its milder forms of embarrassment, fear, or resentment.

There are tremendous negative forces at work that erode people's lives and cause their personalities to deteriorate. But there are also great healing forces at work in the world—and in the depths of our own personalities.

Jesus Restores Dignity, Courage, and Love
As we examine our great need for restoration of dignity,

courage, and love in our lives, we discover the unique healing power of Jesus.

As the Son of God, Jesus brought the divine attributes of dignity, courage, and love into the world and gave them perfect expression in every moment of His life. But He did more than that. In becoming fully human—the Son of Man— He opened Himself to the dark, destructive forces that have torn humanity from the image and purposes of God. He surrendered to the core pain that overwhelmed Mary and has crushed people throughout history. He fully experienced shame, rage, and terror. He *became one with* the hideous abyss of humanity's collective unconscious.

This is why the resurrected Jesus is so wise a guide and so sensitive a comforter. He knows firsthand what it is like to suffer every human discomfort and distress. He knows what it is like to be betrayed, misunderstood, embarrassed, rejected, humiliated, exploited, beaten, and, yes, even killed.

But Jesus did something new. While He experienced fully the poison and agony of being human, He did not give His existence over to it. He did not constrict Himself from the pain of emotional encounter or physical suffering. Rather, He surrendered to it—though it broke His heart and cost His life. He was not overwhelmed with shame or filled with rage. Instead, He bore the shame with dignity and cried out to God for forgiveness of those who tormented Him. In His terror He committed Himself to the wisdom of His Father's care. He endured the terrible inner pain because of the vision of love He had for every person.

Jesus passed *through* the agonizing pain of shame, rage, and terror—His own and all of humanity's as though it were a crucible in which the purity of His own inner core was tested. And He came out the other side filled with joy, peace, and love. In fact, the real story of Jesus is not His crucifixion and death, but His glorious resurrection—the fact that He lives today!

He is therefore a trustworthy guide for finding the deeper purpose of our lives. And He loves us so much because He knows personally how brutal life can be and what Minotaurs of demonic and unconscious forces we wrestle with. And because He never lost for a moment His eternal honor and dignity, He is never threatened by our strengths or put off by our weaknesses. Rather, He delights in walking with us as we become the precious, unique and gifted beings that God originally intended. *He* is the healing power in the depths of *our* being.

How Mary Found Inner Healing

Mary knew at an *intellectual* level that Christ loved her. She knew this from her Christian upbringing. But she did not know it at a *feeling* level because she *felt* ugly inside. And she assumed that God, too, must feel that she was ugly and undesirable because of what had happened with Kelly. She didn't consider that Jesus loved her all the more because of the tremendous stress and suffering to which she had been so horribly exposed.

For seven long, painful years she refused to share the rape experience with anyone—even Jesus. She was polite to Kelly, but never went out with him again. He dogged her footsteps like a hurt puppy. She continued to be a smiling, charming person on the outside. But inside she was haunted by feelings so strong that she wouldn't admit them to consciousness.

It is the honest confession of our problems, pains, and dilemmas to another person or to God that begins the process of inner healing.

One day the pain of repression outweighed the security of keeping everything bottled up inside and Mary came in for counseling. I want to share briefly what happened, because it is a model of how suffering is genuinely relieved and healing imparted.

After seven years of frozen silence, Mary had the courage to retell and, further, relive the rape scene. As she did, her voice captured the hurt, terror, and anguish that she originally experienced. Her body shook, contorted, and tensed.

But then something new and miraculous happened, as it often does when people become radically honest and open for growth. The shame she carried for seven years began to melt away like snow on a hot winter day. It was the warmth of sincere human understanding that enabled her to grow through the shame and embarrassment.

Her voice strengthened and her body loosened up after she surrendered to the intense pain and discovered that it passed *through* her, leaving a sense of peace and well-being in its wake. She faced squarely the pain she had repressed all those years, and found that it did not tear her to pieces. In fact, she felt more whole than before.

The last thing to surface from the unconscious depths was her rage. All the anger she originally felt—and rightly so— began to flow like molten lava from a volcano. With a pillow in front of her as a substitute symbol of Kelly, she beat, and beat, and beat on it until beads of sweat came to her forehead and her arms were exhausted. She screamed at the pillow, clawed and twisted it, and finally put it on the floor and stomped it. Finally a smile came to her face and she said: *"That's* what I really felt like doing when he was raping me...but I was too scared. Now I'm not afraid!'' Then she added, ''It feels good to be mad. He had no right to do that!''

And then the most surprising thing of all. She began to feel sorry for Kelly—and she *forgave* him. ''Think how confused he must be to think that *that* was intimacy. He must live in some kind of hell. I hope that God helps him find himself. I really do.''

When Mary finally got closure on this important ''un-finished business'' of the past, a new harmony began to unfold in her personality. Within the week several friends commented on how radiant her life was becoming. She felt free to hug and touch others, something she had been afraid to do for seven years. She felt more free to be direct and honest in talking to others. She felt more of the existential core of dignity, courage, and love flowing from her inner being. Even her body became more relaxed and graceful.

As we dare to experience our core feelings, the pain we have collected in life is discharged and we allow it to pass freely through us, like electric current passing from a storage battery through a wire and into the ground where it is dissipated.

The liberation of old inner conflicts is accompanied by a release of previously bound-up energy, the energy that was required to repress our feelings and keep us from facing our real selves. The release of inner conflict and pain results in energy that becomes available for healthy growth. We no longer rigidly defend ourselves against the prospect of pain. We dare to surrender to our pain and get it over quickly.

The Importance of Dealing with Unfinished Business

If you have had a moment of betrayal, it is important that you find someone you can trust to tell your story to. As you reveal your betrayal, don't stop until you have tapped all the emotions involved with this particular event in your life— hurt, fear, anger, etc.—even if it takes several sessions. Telling your story to a confidant is vital to you and your emotional and spiritual growth. You will know when you are done because you will feel a peace and a deep heartfelt forgiveness for your exploiter.

As we genuinely face and work through the old unfinished business of the past, a new sense of inner peace and harmony flows into our core. This is known in psychotherapy as "making the unconscious conscious." In Christian terms it amounts to allowing the love of Christ to redeem our entire being, including the light and dark sides of our nature. I like to think of it as reliving old traumas from the past in the present moment, seeking to discover spontaneous and creative solutions to them. Once we hit on the right solution and *do* what we needed to do then but didn't know how, then an equilibrium is restored to our inner being. The awareness that accompanies it is peace, harmony, and joy.

In this process of growth it is important to realize that the unconscious was really on our side all along. It was a part of ourselves which we tried to disown because we didn't understand it and it threatened us. But like a persistent ghost, it kept knocking at the door of our awareness until, with fear and trembling, we let it come in. Psychologist Rollo May says to "identify with that which haunts you, not in order to fight it off, but to take it into yourself; for it must represent some rejected element in you."[3]

When we invite this strange visitor into the warm hearth of our awareness, it sits down to sup with us and give us its message—a message about something in life we have grossly misunderstood or left undone. And suddenly things make sense again. We finally realize that this visitor is no foreigner but rather an intimate part of our own experience. Then we embrace the guest, welcome it home, and seek ways to apply the wise message to our lives. Thank God for the persistence of that patient messenger, the unconscious!

For Mary the inner healing brought a new desire for the joy of an intimate relationship. With practice and determination, she began dating again, only now she worked at being emotionally candid with whomever she dated. She expressed her feelings and values openly. She demanded that relationships be fair and mutual. She refused to get involved in manipulative "come-ons."

Within the year Mary was developing an exceptionally open and growth-oriented friendship with a man who was deeply attracted to the genuine person she was becoming. After two years of marriage they have reported back that they each got exactly what they wanted: an exciting, joyful, honest, growing relationship. For this I thank God.

Whether it is called psychotherapy or faith, all genuine healing is a gift of God who loves each of us perfectly.

Workshop

1. Mary lacked sexual understanding and strength in personal convictions in her relationship with Kelly. Can we remedy this kind of situation in our Christian teachings? How?

What should parents teach their children in these areas?

2. Have you thought about your own moment of betrayal? Have you worked it through yet? If not, who do you know that can help you work it through, someone you trust?

3. Take a moment to become aware if you have betrayed one or more people in a way that has caused them pain. How might you go about bringing healing to them? Could you write them a letter, make a phone call, or pay them a visit? You might become a new source of love, hope and joy in their lives.

4
The Fear of Being Ourselves

For God hath not given us the spirit of fear; but of power, and of love, and of a sound mind—2 Timothy 1:7 (KJV)

In looking at Mary's life in the last chapter we understood immediately that the trauma of rape was the culprit in causing her to shut down the flow of feelings from her inner well. The anxiety from the rape was so intense that the only way she knew to handle it was to block the flow of all feelings, and to put on a "happy mask" to face the world.

We are moved with compassion because we don't want her to have to wear a mask. We want her to be herself. And we are overjoyed when she finally is able to take off the mask and let out her real feelings. Somehow we know that now she can find her way in life. We sense that in being so honest, and in coming to be "in touch" with herself, she will now be able to live life authentically. She will be able to discover what she really wants from life, and to hear what Life is wanting from her.

But Mary is a special instance of a person who spent years

hiding from people because of her deep inner pain.

What about the rest of us who live rather normal lives and have never faced anything as devastating as Mary did? Do we have inner pain? Do we also have tendencies to live life behind a mask? Do we tend to be out of touch with our real feelings and our genuine goals?

It seems to me that the answer is *yes*. I know that the answer is yes for me. What is it for you?

It All Starts in Childhood

Have you ever watched a group of children playing and listened to the kinds of things they say? Children can be marvelously spontaneous. They are so honest and expressive in what they do and what they say. But just as they can be playful and fun they can also be cruel and harsh.

Do you remember the mine-is-better-than-yours game we used to play as children? Somehow we needed to play it to bolster our self-image and gain security in the world. So we found ourselves saying: "My daddy is bigger than yours"; "My dress is prettier than yours"; "My baseball mitt cost more than yours"; and, "The teacher likes me better than she likes you!"

The funny thing is that no matter how old we grow or how adult we think we are, there is still a child in each of us who blurts out these same statements to others. Of course, as adults and especially as Christians, we are much more subtle about it. But we do it just the same. And it's just as destructive now as it was then. It lets us feel good about ourselves because we can feel bad about someone else.

You may be thinking that you are somehow free from the look-at-me and I'm-better-than-you games of childhood. But let me suggest that you may have changed the content of the game without changing its dynamic. So the same game may be played with new themes such as: "I am more generous than other people"; "I have a closer walk with God than

others''; "I am a perfect housewife/business executive/
Christian/etc.''; or, "I am more successful than you."

At any rate, it is quite normal to play such games in our
adult lives. In fact, it is one of the reasons why we are so in
need of Christ's presence in our lives. Jesus stands alone in
His ability to devote His whole being to doing the Father's
will, without being hindered by the subtle need to seek the
praise or acceptance of people.

Jesus loved people but He was firmly resistant to their
demands, expectations, and agenda for His life. He trusted
the inner guidance of the Father in His life enough to make it
His highest priority in every situation and in every
relationship.

Growth Means Trusting Our Heart's Desires

Jesus had something working in His favor we often lack.
He knew that He was accepted by God. He felt continuously
the infinite love and support from God within His inner being.

By trusting Jesus actively in our lives we also experience
the peace, love, and support of God. But as often as not the
bedrock experience of intimacy with God is blocked by our
very human fears—fears that underneath it all we are really
not lovable unless we prove ourselves by striving to be better,
holier, and more perfect than we are.

So we end up trying to find out who God wants us to be by
looking outside ourselves, just as we did in childhood. Only
now it is not Mommy and Daddy that we look to, but instead it
has become our peers, our colleagues, our neighbors, and our
fellow Christians. Criteria are set up by the social or church
groups we join that tell us exactly how we should live our
lives and exactly what goals we should and shouldn't have.
And before you know it we are back in the same game we
learned so well in childhood: trying to impress others and gain
their acceptance and love by doing everything they list for our
perfection. And we are afraid of their rejection if we fail!

The irony here is that while we are succeeding in being the kind of person the world or the church demands we be, we may well be failing in being the genuine person God has called us to be.

Yes, we want the love, support, and guidance that come to us from society, and from church. But what we need to balance that influence is a great trust in the Holy Spirit to work *within* us (see John 16:13).

We do need teaching, correction, and exhortation that Christ provides us through the church and through Christian fellowship. But we also need a deep and abiding trust that God is creating in each of us a unique set of desires, values, and goals that are tailor-made for who we are called to be in Him. The psalmist wrote: "Delight yourself in the Lord; and He will give you the desires of your heart. Commit your way to the Lord, trust also in Him, and He will do it" (Ps. 37:4,5).

What we need to realize is that in not trusting the desires of our hearts, we are not trusting the Lord.

No wonder, then, we end up in later adult years being somehow stiff and plastic people. We have allowed the world to shape us rather than having the courage to allow God to move within us to shape the world.

The growth process that allows us to be ourselves and to become all God intends us to be involves learning to discern and trust our feelings, impulses, desires, intuitions, and values that come like well water from deep within.

To further illustrate the importance of learning to have confidence and trust in the inner well that is at the core of our lives, I have created the following story:

The Littlest Well

Once there was a little well. At least it thought it was little.

Ever since it was created it had been more aware of its "littleness" than anything else about itself.

And the way it learned to judge itself as being so little was by observing all the other wells around it. Night and day it would watch other wells produce their water for thirsty passersby in the valley. The little well knew that these wells had been there for a long time. Many of the other wells had beautiful growths of ivy interwoven around their stone sides and wooden frames over their tops.

This made the little well feel quite inferior, because by comparison its sides were bare.

Then one day the little well decided to put on a new air of confidence and act happy and secure. It beamed with happiness during the day, but at night was overwhelmed with feelings of loneliness and emptiness. Before long it started having regular nighttime depressions and even nightmares. But none of the other wells knew because the little well would hide its secret pain and force a smile and a laugh all day long.

Eventually the little well became fatigued with this plan. It decided it had to try something new to get rid of the feeling of being so empty.

So it told thirsty passersby that they could have a drink of water if they would borrow water from other wells to pay the little well back on their return journeys.

"Surely this will make me full," thought the little well. "By being cautious about what I give, and by making sure I get more water put into me than goes out, I will soon become filled to overflowing and be the talk of the whole valley!"

But this plan didn't work. Passersby began to resent the little well—and even avoid it. And other wells began to warn each other that the little well was a taker, not a giver. The wells knew enough about life to realize that no one could fill the little well.

And, in fact, this is what happened. Even though the little well talked more and more about what a fine job it was doing in the service of people of the valley, in reality it was drying up. The more it tried to use the water from other wells as though it was its own, the more its own core became clogged with algae from disuse.

Finally a desperate day came, and the little well became completely dry.

With great terror and confusion the little well shouted a prayer. "Oh God of the wells," it cried, "please help me! I don't know how to be a good well. I've tried so hard to get enough water to be of service to others. And I've tried so hard to be the best well in the valley. But something terrible has happened. I've dried up completely and now I'm just an empty hole in the ground. Help me!"

That very day the man who had dug and built all the wells in the valley came by.

He was examining each well to see how it was doing, when he heard the cry of the little well. He rushed to the little well with tears in his eyes.

"Little well," he said, "I never meant you to come to this. I created you to be a wonderful well—different than any in the valley. But I never thought in terms of you being 'better' or 'worse' than the others. I only thought of you being the unique well that you are. And the gift I gave you long ago was that I connected you to the same powerful underground stream that brings crystal clear, icy cold water to all the other wells."

When the little well heard this it began crying—only this time for joy. "You mean that the other wells are my brothers and sisters, and that together we are to serve the people of the valley? If only I had realized that before! I've spent my life so far trying to *impress* the other wells, when all I really had to do was *express* myself."

With that the little well relaxed. The man got out some special tools to help dredge the debris out of the little well's core. And soon the little well felt the stirrings from within itself that it had never thought possible.

"I'm alive," it shouted. And it asked all the other wells to celebrate with it that it could now give freely the rich supply of water that was welling up from its depths.

And the wells did celebrate. For each of them had once been a little well. And each had in its own way learned the lesson of being itself, and of trusting the well maker enough to freely give what it had been designed to freely receive.

We Are Like the Little Well

In hearing the story of the little well, we may again find ourselves moved with compassion like we were in hearing of Mary's years of hidden suffering.

Something in the plight of the little well speaks to us because we may see the story as a mirror of our own or other people's lives.

Deep down we don't want the little well to suffer needlessly because of all its fears and insecurities. We don't want Mary to suffer needlessly because of her hidden fears and anxieties. And we don't want to suffer in our own lives because of our own secret fears.

Neither does the Lord, our Creator, want us to suffer the torment of unnecessary and ill-founded fears.

How, then, can we get rid of the fears, or at least begin to break their stranglehold on our lives? Here the Scriptures present a stunning answer: "There is no fear in love; but perfect love casts out fear....We love, because He first loved us" (1 John 4:18,19).

Whether it is by learning to love ourselves, receiving the love of a trusted friend, feeling understood by a professional counselor, or experiencing firsthand the reality that God loves us, love heals our many fears and gives us courage to be ourselves.

In my ministry as a counselor, I seek to build bonds of love and friendship with a person. Healing arises out of the bond of friendship. There is much I have learned in counseling that you can apply to your lives so that you can openly receive healing, guidance, and love from your friendships.

In the next chapter we will explore how friendships give us a safe place to be ourselves and to discover what, with God's grace, we can become.

Workshop

1. Think of a time recently when you played the look-at-me or I'm-better-than-you game. Why did you do it? Was it a good healthy pat on the back or a malicious attempt to make someone else feel bad?

2. In a paragraph or two write a sketch of who you think you are in the eyes of your friends and family. As you look at this picture of yourself do you feel comfortable and *satisfied* with the identity you have established so far? Do those people who have only this picture to draw from see very much of the real you? If not, what can you do to change this?

3. List at least four things about yourself that you like (assets, talents, achievements, etc.). Look at each one and question why you included it.

Do you like this about yourself because it's something your mother or father wanted you to be or do? Or did you aspire to be this because of social pressure? Or are you pleased with yourself for this accomplishment because it is part of God's loving plan for your life?

How can you set your path to follow the desires and goals that most reflect a tie between you and God?

5
We All Need Someone to Trust

Bear one another's burdens, and thus fulfill the law of Christ—Galatians 6:2

It may seem strange to some people to picture a psychologist who one moment would lead a person through an elaborate psychodrama in order to release deeply buried feelings, and who the next moment would lay hands on that person and pray for inner healing and guidance of the Holy Spirit—but that's the kind of thing I do!

I use principles derived from such diverse schools of psychological thought as psychodrama, Gestalt therapy, bio-energetics and behavior therapy. I integrate these approaches with an abiding trust in Jesus and the healing power of His Spirit to touch the particular needs of each person I work with.

In my work as a counselor, what I do from day to day is accept, encourage, and love those people who entrust themselves to my care. In all likelihood they are seeking me out because of a lack of acceptance, encouragement, and love from those with whom they live.

I do exercise skills and techniques that are the tools of my profession. But much of what brings real healing to the person is an atmosphere of genuine love in which, like a frightened turtle, he or she can dare to peek out from behind a rigid, defensive shell.

I have learned in years of counseling that we all become afraid in life. We are all in the same boat when it comes to fear. The things we fear may be different. The degree to which we are afraid may vary. But all of us experience some fear.

Once, in one week's time, a student disclosed to me his fears of not being able to make it in the world, a top business executive said he was afraid of going crazy under the pressure of work, a pastor shared that he was afraid to be open with people, a wife confessed that she was frightened of her sexual attraction to another man, and a parent spoke of feeling anxious that her children would not turn out alright.

I could identify with all of these people because I have experienced these same fears at one time or another. And I still get anxious and afraid about the uncertainties and problems of life.

Being a Christian doesn't mean that we no longer feel afraid. It means that we have Someone to take our fears to and share them with. As Billy Graham says, being born again does not mean that "we will never have any problems. This is not true, but we do have Someone to help us face our problems. The Christian life is not a way 'out' but a way 'through' life."[4]

And it is in this way that I understand my calling as a counselor. I am called to bring healing, comfort, and guidance to people who are struggling to find their ways through life. I draw skill from a broad variety of psychological theories and therapeutic techniques, as well as from a regular assimilation of the Word of God.

Building Core to Core Relationships

My healing alliance with someone is based on our mutual

willingness to be ourselves and to bring our shared resources to bear in the partnership of growth and change. The courage and honesty of many whom I counsel inspires me in my own quest for authenticity. When it seems appropriate I share deeply from my own life experiences. Together we build a "core to core" relationship in which we can both be transparent and self-disclosing. It seems that I have learned most about this model through studying the life of Jesus.

Though His title was, among other things, the Mighty Counselor, He did not come across to people as superior, distant, condescending or judgmental. He came across exactly as He was—humble, honest, relaxed and vulnerable. In so doing, He awakened others to a whole new level of existence that they never thought possible. It was a level that emphasized the unique importance of every person, restored dignity to each one, accepted each person where he was, and sought to impart to each the courage to live a meaningful and exciting life. No wonder throngs pressed in to see and touch Him wherever He went.

Trusting Jesus as my model I approach people who come to me for help as I think He did. If the person I am working with can lose his fear that I might judge or condemn him, then he can gradually open up the most intimate parts of himself in hope of being understood. Perhaps the greatest gift I have to give is understanding—I can accept his secret fears, jealousies, hostilities, depressions, habits, fantasies, and shames.

As this person discovers that he can just be himself with me, he comes out from his many hiding places and starts *being himself.* Now we can work, because in being himself he explores not only the negative in his life experience but also the positive. He shares his hopes, dreams, and aspirations— the most precious parts of him that perhaps others have teased him about or discounted him for cherishing.

In getting it *all* out—the good and the bad, the painful and the joyful, the sorrows and the hopes—we begin to build anew in directions that he longed for, but never knew how to accomplish. I learned long ago from the Lord that a deep hole doesn't have to remain empty. Seen in another light the hole is a foundation on which to build a great building. And a person's pain and frustration can be the hole out of which arises a great personality!

Friendship As a Healing Force

Dr. Sidney Jourard, in *The Transparent Self,* suggests that people become in need of psychotherapy "because they have not disclosed themselves in some optimal degree to the people in their life."[5]

One of the ways that trusted friends can be of great help to each other is to be available for special times of confession, catharsis, and healing. Healing forces are put into motion whenever we sincerely open our hearts to someone we trust. Because we trust them, we can drop all defenses and pour out inner hurts, fears, and secrets of the past.

A trusted friend creates for us a *safe place* in which we can contact our inner pain. He doesn't have to say much; just listen deeply. We are not asking his advice as much as seeking his loving affirmation and understanding of how we feel and what we are.

Old hurts don't just go away. Generally, they need to be worked through with full awareness. That means we relive them and feel their power once again. Our body may tremble, our voice quiver, our stomach feel like it is turning to Jello. But we must stay in contact with the negative feelings long enough to let them pass through us so that we lose our fear of them. As we do so, we are healed because we have gotten rid of the poison that would have numbed our hearts.

In this healing process we need not become like broken records, forever proclaiming the hurts and injustices of the past. Rather, we need to speak it out once and for all, and be done with it.

As we learn to surrender to pain and fear that have accumulated from the past, we discover the secret of inner healing. Like Jesus, we no longer seek to avoid or escape from emotional pain in life. We develop instead the courage to embrace it, wrestle with it, and surrender to it—allowing it to pass through us without leaving us constricted and fearful. Only then does it lose its power to harm us, to render us incapable of loving.

Besides providing a safe place for the sharing of our fears, a true friend gives us opportunity to explore our positive capabilities. A true friend is able to do this because he or she is excited by our strengths, talents, and gifts.

Do you regularly share your weaknesses and brainstorm about your strengths with your special friends? If not, then perhaps this week would be a good time to start. How much richer could the friendship become if you were able to bare more of your heart and soul?

The power of love to heal our fears and inspire our greatness is captured in the following quote by an anonymous author:

Friendship is the comfort, the inexpressible comfort of feeling safe with a person, having neither to weigh thoughts nor measure words, but pouring all—right out—just as they are, chaff and grain together, certain that a faithful friendly hand will take and sift them, keep what is worth keeping and, with a breath of comfort, blow the rest away.

A Core Network of Friends

We each need to take the initiative in developing a core network of intimate friendships. Once we realize how important this is we will free the necessary time and energy to seek friends. If we do not place a high priority on building this core network, then we will travel through life far more lonely, alienated, and disconnected than we need to.

In looking at Jesus we find that He had a core network of deeply intimate friends: Peter, James, and John. With these three friends He was fully Himself, declaring His deepest secrets openly. He also confronted these three friends more than the rest of the disciples. Their deeper experience of His friendship brought with it a larger measure of responsibility. From this intimate inner circle of friends, Jesus extended Himself into fellowship with the Twelve. Here also He disclosed much, though not as fully as with the three. And from the 12 disciples His love radiated toward all humanity.

Like Jesus, we each need an inner circle of friends with whom we can be our whole self. We need to have permission to express ourselves fully, and to let the others do the same. It is in these intimate, long-term relationships that we learn the most about ourselves and about each other. Sometimes we nurture, support, and inspire each other. Sometimes we act as sandpaper so as to rub off the rough edges of our personalities by confronting each other. But through everything we grow to the fullness of self-awareness and self-expression that God intends for us to know.

You can do much to create a positive atmosphere of trust and love with people you live with, people you choose as special friends, and people you work with by using the following principles.

Be available to others to listen, empathize, and express warmth, even when you don't have a solution to their problems. Be very direct in expressing your love and unconditional acceptance of others, even though you occasionally tell them some of their specific behaviors that you disapprove of.

Make it acceptable for other people to talk openly about themselves. You can do this by not being shocked, judgmental, or offended when someone shares something deeply personal with you. Remember the maxim that every human being is worth understanding.

Learn to respond in a mutual way to others in that as they disclose deeper, more penetrating levels of their lives, you reciprocate by opening more of your own life to them.

And last, *learn to be very patient in building strong bonds of love and trust with others*. Don't be so rigid as to demand absolute perfection from them. As human beings we often fail and disappoint one another. The point of love is that we become patient in giving each other many chances to grow and mature in our abilities to become faithful companions.

Trust is perhaps the most important dimension to our relationships with others and with the Lord. It washes away the fears of rejection, ridicule, and betrayal that haunt our lives.

Trust opens the way to friendship, intimacy, and love. It is at the core of learning to love God, and of having the courage to love other people as we love ourselves.

In the next two chapters we are going to talk about another way that you can grow in self-awareness and self-expression, and that is through reading the messages your own body sends to you.

Workshop

1. Early in the chapter the author quotes Billy Graham who says, ''The Christian life is not a way 'out' but a way 'through' life.'' Do you agree or disagree? What experiences have you had recently that confirm or deny Billy Graham's statement?

2. In this chapter the author mentions that he uses principles derived from many diverse schools of psychological thought, such as psychodrama, Gestalt therapy, bio-energetics and behavior therapy. If you know what these methods are, do you agree that they are valid means of helping people toward spiritual growth? Why or why not?

3. The author mentions that we all need someone whom we

can trust. Name one to three people to whom you can completely open your heart, with whom you can drop all defenses and pour out your innermost hurts, fears, and secrets.

4. On a scale of 1 to 10, how do you rate yourself in trusting others?

__I can trust people pretty much all of the time.

__I don't mind being honest with people if they are honest with me.

__There is no point in leaving yourself wide open with people; you'll just get hurt.

6
Love Is Skin Deep

I will give thanks to Thee, for I am fearfully and wonderfully made—Psalm 139:14

Someone once called Jesus Christ "Love with skin on it." I like that because it so clearly shows how *perfect love* from the depths of His being flowed through His personality into the lives of others.

But notice this: it flowed through His hands, legs, arms, eyes, face, lips, and chest. It flowed through His body, which expressed His unique personality. In fact, in his first epistle, John makes a point of saying that not only had the disciples seen the grace and glory of Jesus, but "our hands *handled*" him (1 John 1:1). It was in a very visible and "touchable" way that Jesus manifested the power and the beauty of His divine core.

I have a friend who has worked for 18 years as a clinical chaplain in a state hospital for the mentally handicapped. One day I asked him how he managed to communicate with those retarded people. "I touch them a lot," he said. "You see, words don't mean very much to them. I could talk all day and they wouldn't respond at all. But I've learned to use my body to communicate with them. I touch them with my hands, I caress them with my voice, and I encounter them with my eyes—and they understand. If I really didn't love them, they would be the first to know because they are very sensitive to the unconscious messages others give out. But they sense my love, and they open up to me—each one in his own way.''

In the Christian revelation there is great emphasis that ''the Word became flesh'' (John 1:14). God entered fully into the human experience. The Son of God became a man. How profoundly wise this is. How else could we know what God is like unless He revealed Himself on our own level in ways that we could see, touch, and respond to.

So it is with us, though we may not realize it. The body is vital in understanding and experiencing ourselves. It is not just our thoughts or feelings that count. It is our bodies that other people see, touch, and respond to. And it is our bodies that reveal so freely our inner motivations, our values, and our spirituality.

As Christians we need to learn to express our inner experiencing of life in congruent and spontaneous ways as Christ did. An open Christian has integrated his body with his heart and his words. What occurs deep within is spontaneously expressed at the surface of his skin. He does not seek to hide, defend, or prove himself—only to be fully who he is and honestly express his being to others.

But in our desire to live a full and open life we come face to face with an old dilemma that has often perplexed Christians: somewhere deep within ourselves we feel that our bodies are somehow sinful and evil. This is not only a Puritan tradition, for it goes far back in the Christian tradition. It reflects the feeling that the flesh is the province of the devil, so it is only by abstracting ourselves from the body that we attain true spirituality. Morton Kelsey, in *The Other Side of Silence*, writes:

Our "Christian" religious practice has been largely cerebral for so long that we have built up a sizeable tradition which scorns and rejects the body. We have almost lost any understanding of the relation of the body to the religious encounter. Yet our bodies actually have nearly as much effect on our personalities as the other way around.[6]

Glorify God in Your Body

I wish to suggest that our true spirituality resides *within* our bodies, which are not evil things but specially created vessels through which the grace of God should flow freely into the world. Our body is our earthly "tabernacle." When the Bible says at the beginning of John's Gospel that the Word became flesh, it means that Christ, the eternal Logos, surrendered to incarnation in a human body so that He could "tabernacle" (see John 1:14) among us and reveal the glory of God. And in Colossians we read that "in Him all the fulness of Deity dwells in bodily form" (Col. 2:9). We, in turn, are to be filled by the presence of the risen Christ—bodily. As Paul says, "Your body is a temple of the Holy Spirit who is in you…therefore glorify God in your body" (1 Cor. 6:19,20).

Our bodies are a very important dimension of our being. Our bodies are a primary way that our spirituality is channeled into the world. If we live and work in faith, then we are moved from deep within to do the works of Christ. We become more and more at one with the Father, Son, and Holy Spirit who dwell in the core of our being. Adrian Van Kaam, in *Looking for Jesus,* says:

Out of this oneness flow forth the works of God. He asks us to lend him our eyes to see, our mouth to speak, our ears to hear, our mind to think, our heart to love, our feet to walk, our hands to act.[7]

A full sensitivity to the inner life, inspired by the presence of Jesus within, is blocked because many Christians do not sufficiently *trust* their bodies. For many Christians the head has been viewed as the province of God while the body and feelings have been thought of as belonging to the devil. This mind-body split is not just a problem for Christians. It is also a problem for modern secular man. In our science and business oriented culture we have been taught to overvalue the intellect to the exclusion of emotions and bodily tensions. We have all heard the many messages telling us to ''use our heads'' and not get emotional!

Many of the quests for a more total experiencing of life that characterized the 1960s and 1970s reflect a dissatisfaction with this one-sided approach to life. Sexual permissiveness, experimentation with psychedelic drugs, rediscovery of nature, participation in encounter groups, and fascination with Oriental religions all demonstrate an attempt to regain vital touch with the more intuitive, aesthetic, meditative, and sensual aspects of life. In Christian circles the small group ministry and fellowship of home Bible studies, *koinonia* prayer groups, spiritual growth groups, and marriage enrichment groups reflect this same desire to integrate more of the heart and the body into human experience.

A cartoon by Jules Feiffer illustrates the plight of many people who have not yet discovered that life can be lived with greater vitality and balance by wisely trusting one's whole being.[8] (See p. 63.)

The artificial division of the person into a mind that is ''spiritual'' and a body that is ''carnal'' creates many troubles. It forces a person to live in the realm of words and abstract thoughts. Consequently, one becomes largely unaware of feelings and bodily tensions from the neck down. The heart is blocked out. Sexuality is blocked out. The legs are blocked out. And one eventually is left a hermit in the remote cave of one's ''mind.''

THIS
IS
MY
HEAD. IT THINKS.
IT TALKS.
IT CHARMS.

IT WORRIES.
IT LAUGHS.
IT HURTS.

IT HAS A HUN-
DRED WONDER- I AM PROUD
FUL TRICKS. OF IT.

 THIS
IS
MY
BODY.

IT IS
FUNNY
LOOKING.
IT MAL-
FUNCTIONS. IT LOOKS
BEST IN
WINTER
CLOTHES.

 I HAVE AS
LITTLE TO
DO WITH IT
AS IS
HUMANLY
POSSIBLE.

 LUCKY FOR
MY BODY
THAT I
NEED IT TO
CHAUFFEUR
MY HEAD
AROUND.

OTHER-
WISE
OUT IT WOULD GO.

© 1974 JULES FEIFFER

Yes, we can use our minds as the computer-like instruments they are designed to be. Yes, we can use reason and logic in analyzing data, looking at alternatives, and making choices. But we also need to have profound respect for the more intuitive and sensory elements of our experiences. As Pascal said, "The heart has reasons which the mind knows nothing about." We need the wisdom and support of our whole being—body, heart, and mind—in order to really find our way to joy.

One of the most obvious ways for us to see the importance of the body is to become aware of the many expressions we use that refer to body messages. "You *rub* me the wrong way." "I feel *touched* by your love." "I can't *stomach* this any longer." "He has a kind *heart*." "You give me a pain in the *neck*." "Get off my *back!*" "I don't have the *guts* to go through with it." "She gets under my *skin*." "I won't *stand* for it." "I can *see* right through you." "I'm *falling* in love." "I feel *moved* by your sorrow."

We hear these expressions many times, perhaps without realizing the "down to earth" wisdom of body-oriented phrases. In the Hebrew conception of the soul found in the Old Testament, the soul is made up of the spirit and body together. What that means is that, without a body, man has only a disembodied spirit—and to the Hebrew the very notion was repugnant. For the Hebrews the body was the person, and there was no differentiation between the natural and the supernatural, or the physical and the psychological.

Surrender Your Whole Being to God

Much of growth in healthy Christian spirituality involves learning to surrender one's *whole* being—thoughts, feelings, and bodily sensations—to the will of God.

You may be convinced in your mind that God loves you. But you also need to learn to feel it in your heart and sense it with your body.

The love of God is no abstract thing. It is a living energy that can affect our bodies and our feelings. If we are to serve Him in a wholehearted way, then even the cells of our body, our nervous system, our digestive tract, our respiratory system, our circulatory system, and our body musculature need to learn of His love!

Surrendering our whole being, and learning to live in a more relaxed and trusting way, opens us up to Christ's life in us. Our body needs to learn to feel serene most of the time, because Christ is sovereign in our lives. He brings a real peace to our bodies and to our personalities. Not only that, but He accepts and loves our bodies!

Perhaps in childhood or adolescence someone made fun of our bodies. Because we identify our personalities so fully with how people respond to our bodies, this could have damaged our self-esteem and love of ourselves. We could have shifted our feelings from enjoyment of our bodies to embarrassment over them because someone didn't like them. But this leaves us stuck in a place of fear and shame. It blocks our acceptance of God's love.

But the good news about God's love for each one of us is that He loves our bodies too. He created our bodies and is working to shape and refine our personalities. Just as the "littlest well" (chap. 4) learned to relax and enjoy being itself when it heard that it was loved and valued by the well maker, so we need to learn to relax and enjoy the bodies that God has given us so that we can serve Him without being self-conscious, feeling inferior, or fearfully hiding ourselves.

Our Bodies Are Connected to the Well Within

Our bodies and feelings are designed by God to be in direct contact with the Holy Spirit. Thus, if we are truly desiring God's will to be done in our lives, our bodily sensations and feelings become very reliable ways for sensing His will and doing it.

To constrict our bodies and to numb ourselves to our feelings is to clog the core of the well. This puts us out of touch with the desires of our hearts that God so longs to fulfill.

I was once directing an awareness group that was part of a home Bible study. We would talk about different Scriptures and then apply them to our lives. The goal of our group was honest self-awareness and the expression of our feelings to each other and to God.

In one meeting a woman stated that she wanted to learn to cope with anxiety and worry. It seemed that most of life was one continuing crisis for her. The current crisis was her daughter's wedding the very next week. As usual she was in a real tizzy trying to arrange this and that and the other.

The paradox was that she had asked God to help her, yet everything *still* remained frantic and confused. That's when I noticed her body speaking volumes. Her breathing was shallow. Her shoulders were an inch or two higher than they needed to be. Her talking was fast. Her brow was tensed. And her lips were pursed. The thing that struck me all of a sudden was that this was the way she always looked! Her inner attitudes of insecurity had worked themselves throughout a lifetime into the very warp and woof of her physical being.

I asked her to try an experiment. I invited about seven other people in the group to stand behind her, hands outstretched, and make a human "hammock" for her to lie in. Then I asked her to give up her rigid way of controlling things and "surrender" to the support and comfort of the hammock of arms and hands.

At first she couldn't do it. She worked under the unconscious assumption that she had to do everything perfectly in life, and that things would fall apart without her control. But gradually, and with a good bit of fear and trembling, she leaned more and more on the group until she finally left the floor and was supported entirely by them. As this was happening, I asked her to vividly imagine letting go of all the intricate details of the upcoming wedding to God's wise care—to trust that somehow the really important things would be taken care of, and that the rest didn't really matter anyway.

As she discovered through her own bodily sensation the parallel between physical surrender and spiritual surrender, a wave of peace and serenity came over her. "So this is what it *feels* like to trust God," she whispered. And, indeed, everyone noticed that the frown had disappeared along with most of the other bodily tensions.

I told her to bathe in the sensations so that her body could remind her throughout the week what it felt like to truly trust the Lord. With eyes blissfully closed she nodded. We slowly eased her back onto her own feet.

The next week she told us that the experiment had worked. She had begun to discover throughout the week how she was tensing her body and upsetting herself. With this awareness, she would immediately let go of things and surrender to God, just as she had done that day in the group. Her whole family had commented on how different she was behaving. "I have a long way to go," she said, "but the difference so far is fantastic!"

We need the simple courage to affirm the inner directions for daily living that emerge from our core being. And we need the courage to surrender quietly and firmly to these inner promptings. This is why I emphasize the importance of learning to relax the body and listen to the messages that come to us constantly from our own physical, emotional, and spiritual being.

By becoming aware of your body—looking at it and listening to it on a continuous basis—you heighten your awareness of feelings. Feelings are the private, emotionally colored perceptions that you have at any given moment of life. Feelings reflect your *real* responses to what is going on.

And with increased ability to monitor your feelings and bodily tensions, you come to experience life in a more unified way—heart and mind together, led by the flow of the Holy Spirit from the core of your being.

Teaching the Body to Surrender

I want to suggest that you try an exercise. It is simple, and can have a real impact on your ability to let go of the tension that may be blocking much of the flow of God in your life.

Find a quiet, private place. Perhaps a favorite room in your home. And pick a time of day when there are the least distractions. This is *your* special time.

Now lie down on a couch or on the floor. Get comfortable. Begin to surrender the tensions of your life or of that day—either things you have gone through or things you are soon to cope with.

Think about the Scripture: "Casting all your anxiety upon Him, because He cares for you" (1 Pet. 5:7). Apply that Scripture now by letting go of your thoughts, anxieties, and bodily tensions.

If you become aware of any part of your body that is especially tense, then deliberately tense it more, and then relax it deeply. Scan your bodily tensions from your forehead to the tips of your toes, surrendering deeper and deeper to bodily sensations of deep relaxation and serenity.

Let yourself experience firsthand the truth that underneath are the everlasting arms. *Feel* that assurance, and let it register in your awareness.

At times later in the day or week in which you experience an extra bit of stress or tension, remember these feelings, and how God is closer to you than your own breath. Having experienced emotional and bodily surrender to the presence of God in this exercise prepares you to know how to surrender to His presence in stressful circumstances.

Let yourself bask in the warmth of being deeply at peace

and relaxed. You may wish to pray and pour out whatever is on your heart, just as it is, to the Lord.

When you are finished, gather up your awareness and become fully alert in order to carry out the agenda of the day.

In doing this exercise regularly, say once in the morning and once in the evening, you can greatly enhance your body's experience of being trustworthy, graceful, and sensitive as an instrument for being moved by God's will. You will also develop your emotional capacity to be alive and responsive to what is going on in your life.

Developing good contact with your feelings and your bodily sensations helps you find youself. It also helps you experience more vividly the love of God, and His daily guidance that streams from the core of your inner well.

Workshop

1. The author says that Christians often ''feel that our bodies are somehow sinful and evil.'' Do you feel this way?

Where do you think you got this idea?

2. What do the following Scriptures teach us about our bodies? Genesis 2:7; Psalm 8:5; 119:73; 139:14; 1 Corinthians 6:19,20.

3. Are you aware of what causes tensions in your life? Psalm 147:11 *(NIV)* says, ''The Lord delights in those...who put their hope in his unfailing love.'' What does this mean to you in terms of the things that cause tension in your life?

4. Think of the times you are ''required'' to be phony throughout your average day. Would it be possible to express your true feeling most of the time? Staying true to yourself is so vitally important to your mental, emotional and physical well-being it seems to make sense to try to stay with your initial core feelings as much as possible.

7
Heartstorming

We say that a man is good as his word. With respect we describe him as a man of his word. To achieve this integration, one must start with the body—You are your body. But it does not stop there. One must end with being the word—You are your word. But the word must come from the heart —Alexander Lowen

This is an action chapter. I want to work with you to further develop your awareness, break down defenses, and enable you to open yourself more wholeheartedly to life.

We will use bioenergetic exercises adapted from psychiatrist Alexander Lowen[9] to storm the bastions of your heart by breaking down the defenses in your body. The body, mind, and feelings work so closely together that by focusing for a short time on the body, whole new dimensions of self-understanding and self-expression will open up.

When we are emotionally hurt by someone we tend to draw inward and constrict our entire body. The withdrawal seems to center around our chest and heart areas, as though we were trying to defend our hearts against any further "attacks."

Muscle tension results when we repress our awareness of painful feelings. The pain of repeated or traumatic betrayals in our lives leaves its signature in chronically tensed muscles and in constricted breathing. We try to protect ourselves from future hurts by "armoring" our bodies with muscular tension. But this doesn't really work. Life is to be *lived*, not escaped from. And we can't live if we tie our bodies in muscular knots. If we want to live we must have the courage to again become open and vulnerable to life.

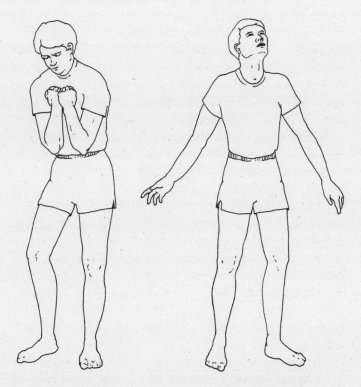

Figure 1: Tense Constriction versus Openness

Try mimicking the pictures you see in figure 1. For a few moments tense your entire body and draw youself tightly inward. Now relax yourself, open your arms, deepen your breathing, and let your heart and chest be exposed. Notice the difference in the two postures. That difference represents two completely different approaches to life. It is the latter more relaxed and open posture that is essential to a vibrant life.

These exercises ought to help you become aware of emotional and physical stiffness. They will also help you limber up the muscular rigidity and replace it with a pattern of deep relaxation. When we truly relax, many positive things happen: we think more clearly; we perceive more accurately; we feel more keenly; and we flow more readily with intuitive guidance that comes from our inner core. This makes it well worth your while to practice these exercises daily for several weeks or months until the wisdom within your body becomes more available for daily living.

Learn to Breathe Correctly

The first step in learning to awaken the wisdom and vitality of the body is to breathe correctly.

"What?" you ask. "Doesn't breathing come naturally for everybody? I've been doing it all my life!"

"But," I reply, "*how* have you been breathing—shallowly or deeply?" You see, most of us started out in life breathing fully. But the more pain and fear we experienced while we were yet growing up, the more constricted our breathing became. When we feel anxious or afraid, we tend to hold our breath. This in turn diminishes our feelings by creating a feeling of numbness. But the cost of this defensive strategy is great. It leaves our body corpselike and our feelings flat.

When we breathe fully, more oxygen is available for the brain and musculature—and more excitation is available for our feelings. This helps us *cope* with whatever is causing our fear and anxiety instead of running away by numbing ourselves.

We need to learn to breathe as a baby breathes—from the diaphragm, in and around the area of the stomach. You can do this by thinking of your diaphragm as a balloon. When you breathe *in,* relax the muscles to such a degree that the "balloon" is able to fill completely. Relax the muscles that criss-cross your neck and chest area as well as those surrounding your stomach.

When you breathe *out,* push out all of the air by contracting the muscles in and around your stomach, thus collapsing the balloon. Remember, be like a baby who has not yet learned to defend itself by tensing these muscles and constricting its breathing.

It may take a conscious effort several times a day for a couple of weeks to rediscover how to breathe in a full and relaxed way. But gradually you will recognize the difference between shallow and deep breathing. You will become more able to "catch yourself" breathing skimpily and correct this spontaneously by taking one or two deep breaths and restoring a rhythm of deeper, more natural breathing.

Breathing is the key to energy metabolism. Improving our breathing pattern is one of the fastest ways to reach positive feelings of peace and vitality throughout the body. In addition to lowering our blood pressure and pulse rate, deep breathing can have a calming effect on our whole personality. We feel less competitive, nervous, and "uptight." We feel more surrendered, more trusting, and more spontaneous.

Ground Your Body

Your legs ground you to the earth. They then support you in your relationships with others. Weak legs or rigid legs are poor supports which cause unstable relationships. Strong, relaxed legs bring the sense of confidence and poise you need for straightforward, gameless relations with others.

The goal of this exercise is learning to stamp the ground in a way that is both firm and relaxed. The firmness symbolizes reliability, trustworthiness, and straightforwardness. The relaxed quality symbolizes openness, genuineness, and fairness in the relationship.

This is a simple exercise, but well worth doing many times. Wearing comfortable, low heel shoes, step to the center of a room, preferably a carpeted one, and begin stamping the floor. Stamp your feet until you feel the muscle strain in calves and thighs. You might try shouting: "I can do it!" or "See how strong I am!"

When the excitation builds to a crescendo in your legs, stop for a few moments and give in to the powerful sensation of being firmly rooted and grounded, just like a big oak tree. Meditate on Psalm 1 which speaks of the blessing that comes to those who ground themselves in their trust of God: "He will be like a tree *firmly planted* by streams of water, which yields its fruit in its season, and its leaf does not wither; and in whatever he does, he prospers" (Ps. 1:3, italics added).

As you stand, sensing the strength of your being pulsating through you, dare to believe in the greatness and potency of your life—it is the gift of a loving God. Then during the day recall from time to time what it feels like to be firmly grounded. Learn to be like the tree: relaxed and firm. Notice how you don't have to tense yourself into a false firmness. The firmness is there if you will surrender and discover it. And that is how it is in life. The firmness of your being is there if you will surrender to it. You don't have to feel inadequate or inferior all your life. You can surrender to your potential for greatness. You can tap the energy for living that comes from deep within.

We have all had our strength and dignity challenged, and this is a good way to teach the hurt or intimidated "child within" that we do, in fact, have a great deal of strength and courage.

Learn to get strong support from the lower half of your body, while still being agile and graceful. With a firm foundation *underneath* you, you can have the courage to contact others with the upper, more expressive parts of your body.

Courage to Be Vulnerable

If we are to live in the present and build *real* relationships with others, then we must open our hearts to the prospect of pain and hurt as well as to the opportunity for love and joy. The grounding exercise emphasizes the *strength* polarity of your being. The vulnerability exercise focuses on your *weakness* dimension. You need to have the courage to be vulnerable—again and again and again. This means you will become willing to stand the emotional pain that will occasionally be your lot in this world of fallible people and imperfect relationships. It also enables you to develop what Rollo May calls the "courage of imperfection." [10] Psychologist Everett Shostrom says that vulnerability involves outgrowing our fear of failing so that we can accept our "fall-ability." [11]

As shown in figure 2, the vulnerability exercise is designed to place your body in a stress position which results in a bodily sensation of pain and a psychological sense of vulnerability and helplessness.

Place your feet with toes turned inward, shoulder width apart. Place a pillow on the floor directly in front of you. Bend your knees until you are in a squatting position just above the floor. Then slowly raise yourself to the position you see in figure 2. Now *hold* this position as long as possible, with your weight on the balls of your feet, before finally falling to your knees on the pillow.

The goal of the exercise is to help you become *genuine* in experiencing and expressing your pain. It also helps you realize that pain, while intense, always gives way to new feelings. As the psalmist said, "Weeping may last for the night, but a shout of joy comes in the morning" (Ps. 30:5).

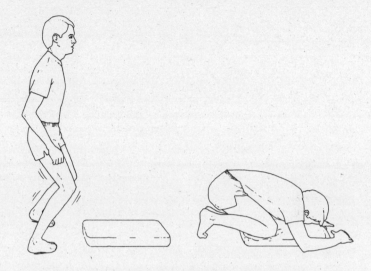

Figure 2: Surrendering to Vulnerability

It is in *bearing with* the pain and expressing it openly that you keep in vital contact with what is going on in life. Don't have a "stiff upper lip" or a phony "smile." Pain is pain and it hurts! Say so. Shout, yell, moan, groan, shake, cry, or scream as the pain increases. Break down the barriers that you have erected to keep from feeling pain in life. Stay with the pain. Embrace it. Surrender to it. And, finally, *exorcise* it by letting it pass through your body as electric current would pass through a copper wire.

When you reach the limits of endurance, surrender to your helplessness and gently fall onto the pillow. The falling itself is symbolic. It represents giving up your rigid system of manipulative control in life, and giving in to genuine encounter with life, God, and others. It shows you that there are no guarantees. There is a price of openness and vulnerability to be paid for the enjoyment and fulfillment of intimacy.

Notice how peace comes to your whole being. It is the peace of having honestly opened yourself up to life—and of having borne the pain that sometimes comes your way with dignity, courage, and hope.

In this exercise you might visualize giving up your striving, controlling attitudes in life, and surrendering to the divine flow of God's will. Losing self-support as you fall upon the pillow reminds you that "the eternal God is a dwelling place, and underneath are the everlasting arms" (Deut. 33:27). Knowing this, you can experience the courage to face pain again in the future without fearfully constricting yourself. If it comes, it comes—you can handle it by owning it and surrendering to it. In the meantime relax and be open to life.

Break Down Muscular Tension

The aim of this exercise is to shake the "starch out of your collar"—to break down muscular tension in the neck, back, and pelvis, and teach you to *flow with life* instead of trying to *control* it all the time.

Place your feet with toes turned inward, shoulder width apart as in figure 3.

Gently form an arch or bow with your back. Stretch your arms over your head and feel the openness to life. As you bend your knees forward you place your body in a stress position in which the natural bodily response is to shake and vibrate. The stronger the vibration the better. Breathe deeply and regularly. Relax your belly completely. Give in to wave after wave of vibrations that pass through your body. The sensation should be pleasant and uplifting like a brook bubbling through the meadow of your inner being.

If you have trouble getting your body to respond to this exercise, keep trying. It could be that you are very tense in the neck and back areas. Most people are. Another possibility is that you are not quite forming the arch correctly. Try experi-

Figure 3: Body Arch

menting as you work to approximate the posture presented in figure 3.

When you slip into the correct position, your body will vibrate spontaneously. Your breathing will have a vibrating quality too, almost like it does when you're standing in ice cold weather. Give in to this and enjoy giving up rigid bodily control in favor of spontaneous body movements. Flexibility in your body aids flexibility in your personality.

Learn to apply the same feeling to daily life. Surrender more to the flow of life and the intuitive (emotional-bodily-spiritual) wisdom that flows from deep within every moment of your life. Learn to trust your body. God created it as a gift to be enjoyed.

Mobilize Your Anger

Most of us were discouraged as children from expressing

our anger. And this is necessary in order to learn to control our impulses because anger can be expressed in harmful ways. But as adults we need to be in touch with anger and express it in behaviors that are gracious, honest and safe. There are constructive ways to handle anger, and everyone gets angry once in awhile; even Jesus did.

Anger is like fire. There are many good things you can do with it. But you have to treat it with respect and caution or everything will go up in smoke!

This exercise should help you get in touch with anger from past or present events. But, more than that, it should enable you to *experience* anger and quit being so frightened or embarrassed by it. Once you become comfortable with your own anger, other people will sense that you know what you're doing when you confront them or strongly assert yourself!

Anger is *not* for the purpose of intimidating, bullying, controlling, or injuring others. Rather, healthy anger is a God-inspired response to injustice, exploitation and manipulation in the world.

As you warm yourself up to being a channel for angry feelings to flow through, you can experiment with gracious, diplomatic, and considerate ways of sharing your feelings openly with someone. It may be your spouse, your best friend, your boss, a relative, or someone you know only remotely. But you can tell him how you feel so that he can understand you better and get his own feelings out. Anger, rightly expressed, has a way of clearing the air of phoniness and opening the door for genuine dialogue.

Anger that you feel but do not express inevitably poisons relationships. It leaves a bitter residue of resentment, hatred, and rage. Anger that you express openly and honestly paves the way for feelings of respect, warmth, and love. Thus the anger polarity swings rhythmically back into the love polarity. A thorough explanation of handling anger in healthy ways is presented in *Healing Love: How God Works Within the Personality,* by myself and Everett Shostrum.[12]

A simple way to warm up to your capacity to express anger in a safe and controlled way is to twist a towel or beat a pillow. Start out slowly, but let yourself give into the feelings as they build. Who is it that has hurt or used you? Let yourself take out on the towel or pillow the full anger that you feel toward that person. Just as David poured his wrath into occasional angry psalms, so you can pour yours into twisting the towel or beating the corner of a bed with a tennis racket, as shown in figure 4.

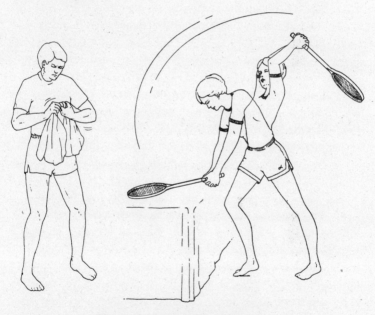

Figure 4: Expressing Anger

This is not a practice for learning to harm someone. It is just being honest about how you feel and doing something physical to get that feeling to pass through you so that you can be finished with it. Sometimes this kind of exercise is like taking the time to drive a nail *all* the way into a plank—a nail that we had pecked and pecked at for years by our crankiness or our complaining. But just hit a good blow and be done with it!

Fritz Kunkel, a Christian psychiatrist, wrote this about expressing anger in his work *In Search of Maturity:*[13]

> You hate your brother: Imagine his presence, before God tell him how you feel, kick him, scratch him …give vent to your emotions. You are ten years old now—get up from your chair, pace the floor, yell, scream, punch the furniture, express yourself. Rant and rage until you are exhausted, or until you laugh at yourself.

> You hate your brother: God is there, tell Him the truth, be as honest as those old Hebrews: "Routed, dishonoured, be they who delight in harm to me!" (Psalm 40:14). Pray God, He should punish your brother, torture him, help you to defeat him. Try to be one with God, the old God of vengeance.

> Look: during all your rage, listening to your furious prayer, God was there, His presence encompassed you like the calm, creative smile of a Father who knows that his child will spend his fury and then discover the truth and find the right way.

Once you have spent your anger—and you may use these techniques many times in life to keep letting anger pass through you—you are ready to follow through to the next step: forgiveness. Anger is not meant to terminate relationships. It is meant to purify and enrich them. So you must have the courage to open your heart again to that person in a wise and loving way. Then your anger will have served its God-given purpose.

Hug Yourself

The last exercise I wish to suggest will probably make you smile.

Hug yourself! That's right. Reach around yourself with both arms and give yourself a warm, loving hug. You would be surprised how deeply we all long to be touched, caressed, and cuddled. Watch any infant or young child.

And as adults we also long to be held, cuddled, and touched—by those people we love and by our heavenly Father. But many of us don't get the daily dose of hugging that we need. Either we're too afraid to let people touch us, or the people we love are too afraid to reach out to us in physical ways.

Why be stingy with our physical expressions of love? And why be uptight about our need to be cuddled? I suggest that you get into the "hug-ability" habit by first learning to hug yourself, then sharing the pleasure of hugging with others who you feel will respond positively to it.

You can give yourself a good dose of hugging by massaging your shoulders, neck, face, arms, belly, and legs. You don't need to feel prudish, self-conscious or embarrassed. *Your body needs to feel loved.* And you can do much to minister to the needs of your body and personality by caring enough about *you* to give yourself some pleasurable cuddles.

Your shoulders have carried burdens, your own and other people's. Your neck has had its share of tensions and pains. Your face has winced with sorrow as well as lit up with delight. Your arms have felt weary. Your belly has been tied in knots with fear. Your legs have trembled with lack of confidence.

Now, with God's love flowing through your own hands, massage, comfort, and soothe all those parts of your body. Feel more whole, more alive, more loved. You might want to do this often in the journey of life. If you learn to love yourself well, then you can teach others to love and respect you. And we all need moments of comfort and love that we feel deeply.

By experimenting with several or all the exercises in this chapter, you can find those that seem most interesting and suitable for you. It is a matter of individual preference. By spending perhaps 20 minutes a day for a couple of weeks or several months—even years—you can greatly enhance your love, enjoyment, and awareness of the body that God has given you.

Learning to love your body and trust your feelings help you to fulfill the second commandment Jesus gave in Matthew 22:39—"You shall love your neighbor *as yourself.*" It helps you fulfill this commandment because *respecting your body and being open to your feelings enables you to learn to love yourself.*

While learning to love yourself is very important, it is only the beginning of true spiritual growth. In the last two chapters of the book, we will look at how to move from loving yourself to loving others and helping to shape the world.

But right now let's turn our focus to the first great commandment: learning to "love the Lord your God with all your heart, and with all your soul, and with all your mind" (Matt. 22:37).

To learn to love God in such a wholehearted and single-minded fashion we need *courage to grow.* And that is what we explore in the next chapter.

Workshop

1. What positive things does the author say happens to us when we learn to truly relax?

Have you experienced an inability to think clearly when you were tense? What can you do when this happens again?

2. Do you feel that you need help in learning to relax?

How much time can you spend each day on these "bio-energetic" exercises?

3. Do you now have or have you ever had trouble controlling anger? Have you been taught that it is wrong to be angry?

The author says that "anger, rightly expressed, has a way of clearing the air of phoniness and opening the door for genuine dialogue." How can you express anger in a healthy way in your relationships?

4. What is the next step for you to take after you have spent your anger? Do you know someone who needs your forgiveness?

8
Courage to Grow

This is my journey of prayer—starting where I am, deepening what I already have, and ever increasingly realizing that I am already there. For the Lord is at the center of my being
—Sister Bernadette Vetter

Miguel, a friend of mine, is a potter. I remember watching him "throw a pot" one day. He took a huge piece of clay, added water to it, and began to turn it on the potter's wheel.

At first the clay was hard and resistant, but as he added more water it became softer and more responsive to the gentle pressure he applied with his hands.

Two things came to mind. He was so strong and muscular, yet he worked the pot so gently. And, although the clay was initially resistant to his efforts, he patiently and confidently kept adding small doses of water until the clay achieved enough suppleness to be worked.

This is how I see the Word of God. It is the water in the clay of our lives.

We live in a culture that is parched and dry when it comes to sensitivity to God. It is easy for us to become brittle and resistant to the flow of God's Spirit. In the twentieth century we are thirsting for meaning, wholeness, and fulfillment. But if our only intake is from secular sources such as the media, the prevailing schools of philosophy, the fads of cultural mores, and the industries of entertainment, then our lives will be too brittle to contain the richness and power of God's will for us.

The Word of God helps to change this. It can begin to slake our thirst. We need to eat and drink the Scriptures—both Old and New Testaments—so that we can assimilate and digest the revelation that God has made about His nature and our nature, His way and our way of discovering His will.

Again, this is a process, just like eating food or drinking water is a process that we continue a little at a time throughout life. But as we continue the process we are nourished in Christlikeness and are transformed from *within* just as Miguel's pots were transformed by the gentle inward pressure of his fingertips.

As Miguel was finishing his pot I was amazed to see him smiling and whistling. He loved that pot! And he loved forming it. And as for the pot, it just needed to enjoy being what it was, while always trusting and surrendering to the process that was at work within it. For it was inevitable that it would finally become the beautiful pot its maker intended.

God Is Our Potter

Reflect for a moment on the words of the hymn we often sing:

> Have Thine own way, Lord! Have Thine own way!
> Thou art the potter; I am the clay.
> Mold me and make me after Thy will,
> While I am waiting, yielded and still.

Where have you felt His touch in your life in the last several days or weeks? How do you feel about being formed by the Lord? Do you find yourself resisting or surrendering?

It is understandable if you find that you are resisting His touch in your life or even if you are confused about whether or not He is there at all.

As I said earlier in the book we all have fears. And one of our fears may well be a fear of God. But if we do indeed fear Him it is because we have not yet discovered how gentle and tender He is. We have not yet discovered how much He is *for* us and how sincerely He seeks to fulfill us.

An important part of growth in our Christian faith is risking trusting God enough times in enough different situations that we begin to become truly convinced of His faithfulness. We begin to find out for ourselves that our *faith* in Him brings a *faithful response* from Him.

If we have not progressed at least this far in our Christian walk, then chances are our beliefs are in a formal expression of religion with all its rules, rituals, and rites, rather than in a living relationship with the risen Christ.

Quite a number of people I counsel have failed to develop a relationship with God because He has at some point in their lives fallen short of their expectations. Perhaps they have lost a loved one in death, suffered a personal accident, or experienced a general sense of frustration about the meaning of life. At any rate they enter into a cold war with God. And though deep down they long to love and trust Him, their faith is blocked by past pain and fear. So they end up spending all their life's energies trying to avoid Him.

Carlos Was Mad at God

I still recall Carlos gazing at me sullenly. He was holding back a flood of feelings—fear, hurt, resentment.

The setting was a quaint psychodramatic stage located just outside Taos. A cadre of university students had gathered for a weekend retreat in the mountains of New Mexico.

Carlos had decided to explore an area in his life that had confused him for years: his feelings toward God. As Carlos looked around the group for someone to play the role of God, his eyes rested on me. He knew from our discussion the night before that I believed in God.

So here we were: face to face. And Carlos found himself sulking. As God, I approached this suave, bearded Cuban.

"Carlos, you want to talk to me, don't you?" I said.

"Yes—no—yes!" he retorted. "Where have you been, God! It's fine of you to show up now, but what about all those years? Why did you leave me all alone?"

"Have I left you alone, Carlos. Or have *you* shut yourself off from me all these years?" I took several steps toward him and stood, arms outstretched, facing him. His arms were tightly folded. His head was bowed, eyes glaring at the floor.

"I wanted to know you so bad as a kid. I needed you. Why did you let me down!" he said.

"The important thing is that we're together now," I replied. "And I have some feelings I want to express to you. How long are you going to mope around? How long are you going to gripe and complain?"

At that I grasped Carlos's arms and began to wrestle him. His surprise turned to anger as he pushed back and yelled: "I hate you, God! You never did what I wanted you to! You don't have a right to be God!"

We continued to jostle back and forth. "Carlos, I like it when you're honest with me. You haven't been that honest in years. I've wanted a relationship with you but you've been a wet noodle. I love you!"

We had fallen to our knees and were now wrestling fiercely on the theatre floor, both sweating and panting. Gradually the grunts and groans began to turn to laughter. Louder and louder it became. We were wrestling and laughing hysterically. The hostility was being transformed into joy. The alienation was being changed into respect and friendship. The suspicion was giving way to trust.

As the psychodrama came to a conclusion we both became aware once again of the 25 people who had shared this intimate baring of the soul with us. Carlos, sitting quietly on the edge of the stage, looked over the audience and said, "Thank you for being part of this. I have found what I have searched for for years. Tonight is a new birth in my relationship with God."

We Wrestle with God Too

The ways that you and I wrestle with God may not be as dramatic as Carlos's struggle, but we share with Carlos some of the same kinds of pain and fear.

What do you do when God confronts you with a rigid prejudice that you have secretly harbored for years? What do you say when God calls you to change jobs, or move to another place, or give up something you were holding onto too tightly? How do you handle it when you or a loved one has an accident or illness—or when someone you love dies? And what about the times when God draws you out of your comfort zone of beliefs, rules, and dogmas in order to show you a larger picture of His love?

What do you do? You wrestle. Just like Carlos did. You wrestle with faith that God will prevail. And because deep down you want Him to guide your life, He does prevail, and you and I are changed. We are transformed in His likeness because we have dared to get close enough to Him to be hurt as well as blessed.

Like Jacob, in the Old Testament, we wrestle with God and leave the wrestling match limping, but abundantly blessed (see Gen. 32:24-31). The limp—the fact that we did not get our way completely—reflects our human limitations. It also teaches us that God alone is God. And that God's way of directing our lives may differ greatly from our own ways apart from God. But it is only through surrendering to His ways, even though it hurts sometimes, that we discover the great wisdom of His plans for us.

After You've Wrestled, Learn to Surrender

Faith keeps us open to God's work in our lives. Even times of confusion, frustration, emptiness, doubt, or alienation can become graced opportunities for prayerful self-assessment, growth in the Lord, and trusting surrender to His unfolding will. It is God arresting our attention through external or internal events in order to bring a new dimension of meaning and purpose to our lives. It is the Master Potter touching us at our points of need that we can be strengthened and made more whole.

In our Christian growth we are not suddenly perfected nor do we need to act that way or feel guilty about our many imperfections. The glory of the Christian is not that he or she is perfect, but that he or she is actively surrendering to the perfect love of God. Our testimony is that we know the Redeemer, the Master Potter, and that we are learning to love and trust Him more as time goes by.

Jesus knows our human faults better than we do. He understands that to be human is to be imperfect, a pilgrim on the way. In Scripture, "perfection" means fidelity, a dependence on Christ, an ongoing relationship with Him. It is with Him that our incompleteness will ultimately be healed and our sufferings will ultimately be swallowed up into joy.

This leads to a sense of serenity—that is, the feeling that with God's help you will always be adequate to the new and novel situations of life. Even when you feel especially weak, helpless and vulnerable, you have faith that an answer will emerge and a solution be found.

Stay on the Road and Out of the Ruts

Rather than living in the emotional ruts of depression,

hostility, or anxiety, we can view our defeats or losses as chances for personal growth. By surrendering to the way things are and trusting God to be the architect of our existence, tremendous things begin to unfold. God can make a desert turn into an oasis. He can make a barren life pregnant with possibility. He can make the ashes of a ruined life rise like a phoenix from the pyre.

The only prerequisite for knowing that it truly is God who is at work in the midst of our trial or painful experience is that, deep in our core, we are giving ourselves to Him. This attitude and commitment involves a real openness to the unfolding will of God. What this means is that underneath my desires, intentions, feelings, thoughts, values, and plans, I have chosen a place of wanting His will to be done in my life even more than I want my own. Never mind that I am still a contradictory, willful, and fragmented person; just as long as I truly long for His will, hunger and thirst for His will, ache for His will to be done—it *will* be done.

But for now we must have the courage to grow. This does not mean copying or imitating Jesus' life as we see it lived two thousand years ago in Palestine. Rather, it means walking with Jesus today—having courage given by the power of the Holy Spirit within to live our lives with as great a fidelity to the unfolding will of God as Jesus lived His earthly pilgrimage.

This is no easy task. The biggest problem is outgrowing our squeamishness about pain. Pain is a healthy and vital part of growth. We should neither seek it nor avoid it, but simply accept it when it accompanies growth. It is often like the travail preceding childbirth. It lasts only a short time, and the joy that follows it far surpasses the pain that was endured.

Do I Trust Jesus More Than Anything?

What happens in the growth process is that gradually we come to trust Jesus in the depths of our being and in every outward circumstance of our lives more than we trust *any-thing* else.

The list of other things we could trust is endless: our dependence on other people's approval; our own achievements; our tightly knit belief system; our convenient prejudices; our inaccurate perceptions of God; our desire of pleasure; our need of wealth or security; our need to be in control; our need to have all the answers; our need to feel helpless; our tendency to become self-righteous; or any other way in which we avoid the ongoing revelation of God's truth to us about ourselves and our purpose in the world.

Because we so easily seek to trust something or someone other than Jesus, we can live in a spirit of gratitude to God that He is constantly seeking us out. And that He won't let us rest until we learn to rest in Him alone.

God is a loving Being. He delights in giving your life the support, inspiration, and provision it needs. He is a God who freely gives life, love, and purpose to all who surrender to His loving will. Jeremiah writes: " 'For I know the plans that I have for you,' declares the Lord, 'plans for welfare...to give you a future and a hope' " (Jer. 29:11). But we cannot know the fruit of greatness without the struggle of authentic growth.

Workshop

1. Think about your image of God. Is it an accurate picture? Do you feel the depth of His love for you? Can you visualize yourself as clay surrendering to His gentle touch? What is He making of you?

2. If your fear of God outweighs your delight in having a relaxed and enjoyable communion with Him, learn to remember to refer to the Scriptures that tell of God's ever tolerant patience and understanding of you. Here are some examples:

God is faithful: Deuteronomy 7:9; Joshua 21:43-45; Isaiah

25:1; Luke 18:7,8; Romans 3:4; 1 Peter 4:19. God is merciful: Psalm 32:5; Isaiah 49:13; Lamentations 3:22; Daniel 9:9; Titus 3:9. God is love: Deuteronomy 7:8; Isaiah 49:15,16; Jeremiah 31:3; Hosea 11:4; Zephaniah 3:17; Romans 8:38,39; Ephesians 2:4. *Keep your picture of God biblical* and not bound with earthly prejudices as to His limitations.

3. Think of the last time you received a painful change in your life plans from God. Try to remember the hurt you felt at the time. Then follow the event through to its eventual outcome in your life. Did you grow as a result of the experience? Can you see now what God saw all the time? Try to make this mental image of God's love and faithfulness strong enough to help you through your next trial.

9
Values to Grow By

But when He, the Spirit of truth, comes, He will guide you into all the truth—John 16:13

Using the well as an analogy for the personality, we have focused in previous chapters on how to prime our inner well with the love of God, and how to keep the core of our well free from the clogging factors of pain and fear.

In chapters 6 and 7 we looked at how the love and wisdom of God *flows* through our own bodies and feelings. In chapter 8 we explored the dynamics of the *growth process* involved in learning to love and serve God with our whole being. Now we will expand the metaphor of the well by concentrating on the inner *walls* of the well which direct and channel the flow from our inner cores out into the world.

The *flow* consists of our heartfelt emotions, our gut reactions, our creative intuitions, and our inner promptings from the Holy Spirit. The *walls* of our inner well are formed by the thoughts and assumptions that we have about life, that is, our *personal values*.

We each have a philosophy of life—a set of assumptions

about life and a structure of values which gives consistency and meaning to our behavior. The question is: Is our philosophy made of straw and mud or is it made from stone or mortar? It makes a big difference! And, further, are the walls of our inner well thrown together in a haphazard way or built with much time and care.

Poor values give us a faulty foundation for living. Good values shore up the walls of our inner well and enable God's energies in our personalities to flow readily into the world.

In this chapter I will suggest some values which I believe foster personal growth, fidelity to the Lord, and healthy interpersonal relationships. These values are open to expansion and revision, but for now they reflect the most reliable guidelines that I have gleaned from psychology, the Christian faith, and life itself.

Perhaps these values will stimulate you in your own quest for values to live and grow by.

The values that we will explore include: developing a sense of mission in life; becoming inner directed; not playing God for other people; forgiving others; being sensitive to others; being a living channel for God's work.

A Sense of Mission in Life

If we do not feel worthwhile and significant, we become restless, hostile, cynical, or bored. We have a deep instinctual need for our lives to make sense.

Here we must leave room for some paradox and mystery in our attempts to formulate values and goals in life. We actively seek meaning and purpose, but not to the point of being brash. Can you picture for a moment storming the gates of heaven, grabbing God by the collar, and demanding to know the meaning of our existence—right now! No, we need the qualities of patience and gentleness mixed in with the persistence of our seeking.

But, on the other hand, we don't want to become so

apathetic that we let life slip through our fingers without having ever *lived*. A common way that life can slip through our fingers is that we live out our own or someone else's dream for us without truly having gotten that dream from our relationship with the Lord. When we do this, we end up living a far more limited and narrow life than God originally intended.

Dave was a student in my group dynamics class. Perhaps by looking at Dave's experience of having his personal dream shattered only to discover deeper meaning in life we will have the courage to take a closer look at our own values.

Dave had to face what many of us go through from time to time. He spent his life developing his potential as an athlete. Everything in high school and college was subordinated to the aim of becoming a professional football player. Just as he was drafted by the very team he wanted, he suddenly came down with hepatitis. When he recovered from the ordeal the doctors said he could never play football again. His world crashed around him. As he bore his broken heart to our group we all felt deeply touched by this reversal but there was nothing we could do except offer our comfort.

For weeks he was restless, alternating between extreme depression and extreme anger. He felt betrayed by life. After several months, though, his attitude began to change. "I wonder what Life is asking me in all this?" he said one night. He began to surrender more to what might be the deeper meaning of his situation. Then insight started to flow. "I'm beginning to see how narrow my life has been. Everything has centered around football. I haven't developed anything else. I don't know how to have good relationships with people. I don't know how to handle my feelings. I don't know how to think about anything that's not related to football. I believe Life is telling me how much I'm missing!"

In the weeks that followed, a remarkable change occurred in Dave. His rage mellowed. His rigidities melted. He began to discover the world of people and relationships that he had been oblivious to throughout life. He began to restore love and discipline to his marriage, which was in such bad shape. In fact, he "discovered" his wife! He had for several years been unaware of her as a person. Everything had centered around football. There had been no room for her. She responded enthusiastically to his new love and attention.

And, last, he began to discover a relationship with God. Somehow in all the disappointment and shaking of the foundations of his life he sensed the quiet companionship of One who loved him. He had never had time for God. But he began to make time for this new relationship—and the love and strength he drew from quiet times with God had a noticeable effect on him. Still, the hurt of not being able to realize his childhood dream lingered, but more and more a new hope and positive trust in the future took its place.

One of the important things we can learn from Dave is to put a high priority on our quiet openness to God. You might prefer a "prayer closet," daily devotionals, regular Bible studies and group sharing, long walks alone with the Lord, or some combination of all of these. But it is so important to spend enough regular time being open to Him so that He *can* influence our dreams and create our heart's desires. *Then* our goals in life become more trustworthy from the beginning.

When it gets right down to it, you—alone with God—must choose what you will become. Life offers both possibilities and problems. Each of us has both potentials and limitations. We need to set about negotiating with reality to discover what our mission in life is and what practical ways we can go about developing and expressing our special gifts and talents.

Being Inner Directed

When we feel so insecure in ourselves that we will do anything to get others' approval, we are in trouble. This is a servile position that makes us prone to being manipulated and controlled by others who do not know how to love and affirm us. They control us by hanging the carrot of their approval in front of our noses as though we were donkeys.

They promise us praise and admiration if we prostitute ourselves to meet their whim and fancy. We give up our birthright of dignity, courage, and love in order to live up to their expectations and demands. We lose our God-inspired direction in life by seeking to please them.

Those who would try to manipulate us in this way might include parents, spouse, relatives, friends, colleagues, boss, or children. On a larger scale, even church and state may fall prey to manipulating us to serve their own ends.

When we give in to these demands from outside ourselves, life becomes very frustrating. We are literally backed into a corner and have no room to breathe, to move, or to grow. We constantly feel ''watched'' and ''judged'' by the person or persons to whom we have given the power to direct our lives. We are shattered by their criticism and relieved when they finally throw us a crumb of approval. But is this any way for a human being to live?

To get out of the corner and back into the mainstream of authentic living we need to learn to give up our childish need for their approval. We must decide that we have innate worth and value, and a destiny of our own. In a word, we must learn to love and respect ourselves. As we are weaned of our infantile dependence on someone else, we gain strength and confidence to trust our own judgments. We trust the flow of wisdom from our own inner being. We come home to our feelings, thoughts, and bodily responses. We realize that— with God—we are adequate to the task of living, growing, and choosing. If we fall flat on our face, we can get up again. If we make a mistake, we can rectify it. If we make a foolish choice, we can become wiser for it. We lose our fear of living and instead gain the *courage to live*.

This results in a sense of "being together" at the levels of thinking, feeling, and bodily response. It is having the courage to relate to the world with my total being—who I really am and who I feel called by God to be.

Don't Play God for Other People

The other side of the coin of self-responsibility is the awareness that other people, too, have the responsibility of directing their own lives. Untold misery, frustration, and suffering come to us when we try to play God in someone else's life. If we truly love someone, we learn to *trust* their own capacity for growth and self-direction. We "take hold" of them by our loving concern, but "let go" of them by our wise detachment. We must let them experience life and learn from the consequences of their choices. If we are constantly snooping, advising, or rescuing them, they have no opportunity to gain the confidence and strength of standing on their own feet.

If we do not learn how to wisely let go of others, then we easily fall into the trap of contaminating our prayer life by demanding that God make them into the exact kind of persons we think they should be! And we frustrate ourselves terribly while waiting for Him to do it.

How much wiser it is to give people over to God's loving care. Perhaps they do need to change and grow. Perhaps we are even correct in what we believe needs to happen in their lives. Even so, we can never force them to be what we think they should. This only builds frustration and resentment. We can only turn them over to God's care, trusting that He will enable them to find the right direction for their lives—whether or not we understand or agree with that direction.

Here, then, is the maxim: I can take responsibility only for my own life. In regard to others, I can tell them how I feel about their life or behavior, but I can never change them, nor should I feel responsible to do so. I can exercise my faith in trusting God to wisely direct our lives, but I should not be so brash as to demand exactly how He should go about doing it. I need to become deeply open to God's own method and timetable for bringing about constructive change in my life and the lives of others.

Be Forgiving

One of the wisest things we can learn to develop is the ability to forgive others. There is no doubt that we will be abused, exploited, and manipulated many times in life. And it will become so tempting to let hurts, pain, and fear stop up the flow of love from our well within. But it's not worth it.

Life is too short and too much of an adventure to allow ourselves to become poisoned with the bitterness of holding a grudge or wasting energy seeking to pay someone back for their wrongdoing. As Paul suggests in Ephesians 4:26 we should have the wisdom to get over our anger quickly—the very hour or day that it happens. Letting it drag on and on just exhausts us.

Sometimes it can be difficult to forgive someone who has injured us. But if we realize how carrying a load of resentment is like physically carrying around a big rock, we understand the wisdom of dropping that load and getting on with the important things in life.

Many people have difficulty forgiving those closest to them, especially their parents. But it is essential that we forgive our parents and learn to love them. We may disagree with them. We may find shortcomings in what they did or didn't do to us. But we must realize that they too had deficits in their personalities and blind spots in their understanding of life. It is part of being human. They too have suffered. We don't need to add to it with our accusations. We can be honest about our anger if we indeed feel that they have harmed us in some way. But we must quickly get over the anger by expressing it in some constructive way and then committing ourselves to the task of learning to understand, accept, and love our parents.

I recently received a letter from one of my students, Anne, who had been struggling to put her relationship with her mother on a more solid foundation. As the last child in a family of seven children, she often felt left out of the family interaction. She was the last one to ever be considered or even talked to.

As a 20-year-old college student, she now realized that she had bottled up a lifetime of hurt feelings that needed to be dealt with. Her letter expresses her courage to work through her hurt and angry feelings in order to have a more loving friendship with her mother.

From Anger to Forgiveness to Love

"I was mad. Mad at life, people, places, and God. But mainly mad at myself. I didn't know why I was feeling this anger, but it swept over me like a tornado as I rode home from school.

"I wanted the intimacy I had been hearing about. But all I had was this anger. I felt like there was a little girl inside of me who had built a wall to hide her many feelings of pain and sorrow. That little girl would deny that they existed—to others, to God and even to herself.

"My whole way of life suddenly seemed like a stage in which I played a part and had never truly been myself. I had never experienced honesty and openness—at least not fully. But why was I feeling so angry?

"I arrived home and everything started off wrong. My mom and I started to bicker and argue back and forth. We hadn't done that for a long time. The anger kept building and building, but I couldn't express it openly. I thought to myself, *Why won't she let me get rid of this anger!*

"I left the house and walked to the top of the hill. Yet even there alone with nature I couldn't find a release. *Nobody will let me get this anger out!* I thought.

"Then it hit me: *I* wouldn't let myself get rid of the anger. It wasn't anyone else. It was *me* who was holding the anger inside. I could no longer blame anyone else. I had to take responsibility for my feelings.

"I went back to the house still feeling angry, but confused as to how to express it. You just didn't express anger directly in our home.

"The next morning I woke up with the same angry feelings. I felt like I was going to burst if something didn't happen. Later that morning I was standing by the heater when my mom said something to me. I don't even remember what it was but the dam inside me burst and a flood of resentful feelings came out.

"I started crying and yelling at my mom: 'Ever since I was a child I've never felt like you loved me. You never had time for me. I was a little girl in a big confusing world with a lot of people bigger than me, and nobody had time for me! Not you or anyone!'

"My mom started crying and yelling back: 'I did my best. What else could I do?' Then she ran out of the house.

"I dropped on the floor sobbing, and thought to myself: *Here we go again...another time I need you and you walk out on me. All I want you to do is show me you love me, but you leave me instead.* And I lay there crying.

"Then Mom came back into the house and I said, 'Mom, will you come and just hold me and let me cry? I want you to hold me.' And she said, 'I wanted to but I didn't know if you wanted me to.' So we sat there on the floor and we hugged and cried. I told her all about that hurt little girl who had tried to be strong and not let anyone know she was hurting. And we cried some more.

"Then we prayed. We prayed that Jesus would heal the hurt and replace the pain with love. Then I said, 'You know, Mom, ever since I was a little girl I've always wanted to go into the kitchen and bake a pie with you.' So we went into the kitchen and baked two pies!

"I realize now if I had told Mom that I needed her before, she would have been there for me. If I had shared the struggles and pain she would have shared them with me. But I held it in and she hadn't known how badly I needed her.

"I've learned a lot by the experience we shared that day. Not only is our relationship deeper and closer, but I have a deeper longing to share the same openness with others."

Do You Have Unfinished Business with Your Family

We all have strong desires for peace, love, and support among our families. It is not always possible to have the harmony and friendship we desire with family members. But to the extent that we do not have peace we will probably have either a cold or hot war with them.

It's not easy to be parents. Most parents truly love their children but may have never learned how to express their love adequately.

The same goes for children. It's hard to be a child. And many children do not learn effective ways to actively love and appreciate their parents.

It is also difficult being a sister or brother. Because siblings most always have some kind of rivalry for attention and love from parents, most brother-sister relationships have a good deal of jealousy, misunderstanding, and even bitterness in them.

So we *all* need healing! And we need to work through our past hurts or resentments in order to move on into relationships that are filled with caring and enjoyment.

A good place to start is in our prayer life, asking God, who longs for family unity more than any of us, to teach each one in the family how to be more honest, more open, and more loving. And then we need to trust *that* prayer as God answers it over our lifetime.

If you find that you are really stuck in a miserable relationship with one or more family members, then perhaps the following exercise will help break the logjam and get things moving again.

I have structured the exercise for dealing with your parents. But if you feel reasonably satisfied with how things are between you and your parents, then I suggest you do the exercise with someone else in mind—a family member, a teacher, a coach, a spouse, or whoever you are harboring real resentment toward.

Sit with pencil and paper and write an "Open Letter to My Parents." You will not send this letter to them, so you can feel free to express yourself openly. Start by telling them about the core pain they have caused you—how you felt ignored, teased, spoiled, deprived, discounted, used, embarrassed, intimidated, smothered, or abandoned. Get all your feelings out, just as they really are.

Now become aware of the problems your parents had and tell them you want to understand them better. Explore how the war, the depression, the wrong choice of a marital partner, the lack of understanding about life, the burden of raising a family, or a poor experience when they themselves were children left them unable to give you everything you needed. Feel empathy for the frustration, confusion, and deprivation they have known in life. Feel for them in the many needs they had that were not met, and in the many tears they shed in the course of life. But be aware that with what they had they did the best they could.

As you are doing this ask Jesus Himself to illumine your memory and bring to your awareness any unfinished business from the past. Ask Him to facilitate the healing process and to enable you in the future to build more loving bonds with family members.

Now courageously assert yourself in forgiving them. Write down some specifics: "I forgive you for being so tense and stern when I was little''; ''I forgive you for not listening when I needed to talk things over''; etc.

Now end the letter by telling them of the kind of relationship you want in the future. Describe ways in which you want to express your love to them. Tell them how they can show their love to you. Now turn your back on the old hurts and resentments and close that chapter of your life forever. You may want to keep this letter in some safe place or you may want to throw it away. You may even want to share it with your parents or whomever you have written it to as a catalyst for discussion and growth. Do what seems right to you.

People, Not Things

Instead of a life based on taking, we need to develop a life-style based on giving. This may sound like a radical statement. It is. It goes against the grain of most of our cultural upbringing which teaches us to get, win, and take. The phrases ''get ahead,'' ''win at all costs,'' and ''take all you can'' should have a familiar ring.

It is so easy to suppose that the meaning of our lives is revealed in the possessions we own, the popularity we enjoy, or the stimulation we experience. But when all the dust of our busy lives has settled, none of these things bring inner peace, harmony, or joy.

It is the *quality of our relationships,* not the quantity of our material goods, social acquaintances, or titillating experiences that count. This is the message that we in the Western world need desperately to understand.

In giving we are deeply ''full-filled'' or filled again and again to overflowing by the love of God which wells up within us like an underground stream. In fact, it is the *giving* attitude that enables our deepest nature to be fulfilled. A giving heart is a heart sensitive to the heart of God. It is a heart open and sensitive to the deepest needs of humanity as well. It is a heart that is not constricted or hardened in spite of the pain experienced in the journey through life.

The power of the Kingdom of God at the core of our lives generates behaviors such as cooperating with others for a common good, sharing possessions, sacrificing when love requires self-denial, and genuinely caring for the well-being of people.

Be a Channel for God's Love

The guidelines for a Spirit-inspired approach to life are not easy to live by. In fact, they may well be impossible to live by on our own. We need to be in intimate contact with a Source greater than ourselves to draw strength and wisdom for living this way. James' Epistle in the New Testament gives us an important word: "If any of you lacks wisdom, let him ask of God, who gives to all men generously and without reproach, and it will be given to him" (Jas. 1:5).

In a Christian's life that source is the Holy Spirit—our own personal Comforter and Counselor whom Jesus imparts to us as an intimate companion for the journey through life. Jesus said that the Holy Spirit would abide within us and would daily give us everything we need for living the best life possible. He also said that the Spirit within would guide us in truth and give us inner courage to live a life based on faithfully serving the Lord (see John 16:13).

Surrendering ourselves each day to the Holy Spirit enables us to draw directly from the richness of Jesus' own personality. His power flows through us and into the world through the unique dimensions of our own particular personality.

Just as there are many different sizes and types of wells that effectively channel water from the earth's depths to its surface, so there are many different types of personality and styles of personal ministry among those who tap the power of the Holy Spirit.

What all of us who desire to serve the Lord have in

common is the one God who desires to flow through our lives in order to touch, heal, and redeem His world.

Workshop

1. What is your occupation? Is this job leading you toward your ultimate mission in life according to your inner promptings and God-given talents?

If it isn't, what efforts do you have time and energy to put into action at this moment to begin redirecting your vocational path? An appraisal of God's gifts to you and your ability to use them is essential to the goal of staying in tune with God's purpose for your life.

2. Do you have an overly developed need for praise and admiration from those around you? When an opinion is requested of you while you're with a group of friends, do you adjust your opinion to fit the situation or do you feel free to say what is in your heart?

3. If you have problems with question 2 the odds are that you will have greater difficulty remaining true to your values (or often remembering what they are for that matter) and will be easily led astray from the mission in life that God brought you here to accomplish. Because of the importance of this matter, sit down right now and make a list of at least 5 values that you do hereby commit yourself to in the future. Then work to expand *and revise* (for we all change) this list regularly.

10
The Journey of Love

By this all men will know that you are My disciples, if you have love for one another—John 13:35

Learning to love is the single most important task of life. We need to put a high priority on doing it.

Learning to love is like learning to ride a bicycle, play sports, or speak a foreign language. It takes time, energy, and practice—lots of practice!

Does it seem strange to hear that we need lots of practice in learning to love? Yet, how else can we learn to be open to others, to be sensitive to them, and to desire and work for their well-being. Loving someone involves various skills. Yet, many people feel that loving is simple.

Let me make a distinction here. "Falling" in love is simple. "Growing" in love is what is hard. By falling in love I mean becoming infatuated with someone in an unstable, self-centered way. Even the phrase "falling in love" implies lack of balance. It is the person who is basically unstable and who does not really know how to love that *falls* into love. He or she falls in love the same way one falls into a ditch or falls off a bike—by not paying attention to what is really happening.

To choose to grow in a loving friendship with another person who at the same time is choosing to grow with you is what loving is really about. Quite the opposite of falling in love, *growing in love* requires emotional balance, realistic assessment of one's self and the other person, and accurate communication and agreement about how the love commitment is developing.

True love and genuine friendship are not accidents. Therefore the phrases "being swept off your feet," "falling head over heels in love," "losing all your sensibilities," and "being madly in love" do not apply to a truly loving relationship. They do apply to a hysterical, volatile, and very unreliable relationship.

A truly loving bond between two or more people is chosen gradually and deliberately, with full awareness and respect for your feelings and theirs. It is this quality of loving that is the subject of this last chapter.

Love Is a Passageway

Love is the doorway through which we pass from solitude to kinship with all humanity, from selfishness to service and companionship. Our passage through the doorway of love may include all of the fear, pain and travail of our original passage through the birth canal into this world. And the result is just as revolutionary: we are delivered into a whole new experience and understanding of life.

In order to nurture a good many relationships in our lives that are truly loving we need to expand our understanding and use of the phrase "I love you." It really means: "I am willing to be fully present in a relationship with you. I care what happens to you as years go by. I want to contribute something to your life, and I am willing to open my own heart to receive

deeply from you.'' This is the mark of the growing Christian.
But this is not an easy pathway to follow.

An extended passage from Gibran's *The Prophet* beauti-
fully illustrates the courage it takes to become a true disciple
of love:[14]

When love beckons to you, follow him,
Though his ways are hard and steep.
And when his wings enfold you yield to him,
Though the sword hidden among his pinions may
    wound you,
And when he speaks to you believe him,
Though his voice may shatter your dreams as
    the north wind lays waste the garden.
For even as love crowns you so shall he crucify you.
 Even as he is for your growth so is he for your
    pruning.
Even as he ascends to your height and caresses your
    tenderest branches that quiver in the sun,
So shall he descend to your roots and shake them in
    their clinging to the earth.
Like sheaves of corn he gathers you unto himself.
He threshes you to make you naked.
He sifts you to free you from your husks.
He grinds you to whiteness.
He kneads you until you become pliant;
And then he assigns you to his sacred fire, that you
    may become sacred bread for God's sacred feast.
All these things shall love do unto you that you may
    know the secrets of your heart, and in that
    knowledge become a fragment of Life's heart.

Love Is Expensive

It might be wise to weigh the cost of becoming a truly

loving person before we commit ourselves to that end. What must it be like to climb the steep mountain of love, to be stabbed in the heart, to have some of our dreams shattered, to be pruned, and to have our very roots shaken? Are we willing to surrender to the lifelong process of being threshed, sifted, ground and kneaded into the kind of person who is truly like God?

For God is love. He gives blessing to those who serve Him and to those who rebel against Him. He seeks the companionship of those who adore Him and those who despitefully use Him. He opens His heart to those who bless Him and to those who curse Him. And His own heart has been broken many times.

But for the person who follows the pathway set before him or her by love, the reward will be inner peace and joy along the way. The essence of the Christian life is *trust* in the Father's love. He has seized us by His love, adopted us as His children, and energized the core of our being with His Spirit. He *delights* in guiding us along the best pathway of our lives. He ties together in meaningful continuity our past, present, and future. He carefully integrates our lives with the Life of the cosmos. He comforts us with the companionship of the Holy Spirit each day. And the Father sends the Son, Jesus— to whom we can relate as a brother and friend—to show us the way of love from deep within.

Like trees in an orchard we must give that we might live, for to withhold is to perish. And in the analogy of the fruit tree we learn a profound lesson. The more the tree is pruned back and cared for by the gardener, the more the tree is able to give. The more it gives, the healthier and hardier it becomes, because it is fulfilling to the utmost its purpose in life.

By giving liberally the fruit that mysteriously appears on its branches it fulfills its true purpose in life. It did not strive to make the fruit appear. Rather, it surrendered to the action of sunlight, soil, and rain. By surrendering to the growth process, it bore fruit abundantly when the season came. So it is with us. Jesus said: "I chose you, and appointed you, that you should go and bear fruit, and that your fruit should remain" (John 15:16).

Love Starts at Home

We can best continue the long journey of learning to love by admitting how truly difficult the path is and how hard it is for us to be loving persons. Let's start with our own families. How many times a day do you hug, smile at, encourage, listen to, and appreciate the members of your own family? How many times a day do you tell family members or other close friends that you love them?

"But they should already know that," you say. Really? *How* will they know unless you tell them and show them time and again. "But we never showed our feelings openly when I was growing up," you reply. Perhaps that is why you find it so difficult to express your feelings fully now. But with practice you can learn to. It will make a big difference in your relationships.

In Keith Miller's book *Please Love Me,* the protagonist, Hedy Robinson, asks the stirring question:

> I couldn't help wondering if there weren't families somewhere in which people told each other every day about the love they felt and hugged and kissed each other—where people shared their hopes and dreams, their difficulties and fears at the dining room table. I tried to imagine our doing that, but couldn't. As long as I could remember, I'd wanted to express my feelings of love and affection to people close to me. But the greater fear of being rejected always kept me from it. [15]

Does the frustration that Hedy experienced in wanting a more supportive and loving family life sound familiar to you? Does it stir a longing in your heart? How high on your list of priorities is having a family in which there is a free exchange of hugs and verbal "I love you's?" How deeply do you value being around to share your hopes and dreams, your triumphs and failures with family members, and to let them share freely with you?

If you do long for genuine warmth and intimacy with your family—whether it is your parents, or whether it is your own spouse and children—you need to know that it does not come easy. Loving takes much courage, much commitment, and much energy. Only if you are willing to devote yourself sincerely to learning to love and to communicate with family members can you enjoy the fruits of that love.

An important principle for building loving bonds with those in your family is to realize that none of them can read your mind. If you love them you must say so in very direct ways. If you want them to know how to channel their loving feelings toward you, you must be willing to express how they could best do that. They won't know how to show you love unless you help them to learn. And, likewise, you can ask them often how to develop new ways of showing your love to them.

The ways we can learn to express love to each other are endless. For one person getting an occasional bouquet of flowers has very special meaning and conveys great tenderness. To someone else the flowers mean very little, but a person who listens respectfully to them when they share intimate feelings conveys love. For one person the fact that you watch for material things that they need and want, and that you surprise them with a special gift every now and then shows that you care. Yet to another person, material gifts will never go very far in showing them that they are loved. What they may want is your quality time in doing things with them, or having regular times for conversations. The list goes on and on.

So you can see why it is important for you to really get to know the people you love and to learn to keep up to date in knowing their desires, wants, needs, hopes, dreams, sorrows, frustrations, and special joys. Only then can you become a vital part of their lives in a loving way.

And the same goes for teaching others how to love you. By risking letting them know you better and better you show them who you are and what you need to find fulfillment in life. You may have to do this gradually in order not to overwhelm them.

None of us can legitimately overload someone else in our desires to have them love us. That would amount to making them God in our life. It would also be unfair to them because when it comes right down to it, one person cannot *make* another person happy. We are each responsible for learning to make ourselves happy. Through a growing awareness of what we need to help us find joy in relationships and fulfillment in our life missions, we can share our needs with those we love and trust. But no one can take God's place in being our ultimate source for guidance, fulfillment, and joy in life.

God wants us to have a blessed family life, not so that the family will take His place, but rather so that the family will become His instrument for healing, guiding, and loving the members of that family.

Expanding Your Circle of Love

We can learn much about ourselves through our families. We can also develop skills of empathy, communication, and love by learning to work through conflicts or problems, and growing into deeper levels of understanding and relating to each other. The family is a great place to be doing this because in our families we feel more of a lifelong kinship and bonding than with other people.

But the family is only the beginning of loving relationships. As soon as we are able, we need to exercise the courage and trust to move out of our focus on loving family members into a larger circle of feeling kinship and love with a growing number of people.

A healthy family life is a springboard for jumping into meaningful, enduring relationships with more and more people. The people may be our neighbors, work associates, school friends, church friends, or even strangers whom God brings into our lives.

Without the process of always being open to relationships with people, we tend to stagnate in a small, in-group of friendships. Being cliquish in our tightly defined circle of friends runs counter to God's love of all people. It shuts us off from the many new ways of experiencing God, life, and people that would come freely if we were more open and caring toward humanity in general. It also locks us into our narrow set of values, prejudices, and beliefs.

By being willing to risk friendship and love with new people we become open again to fresh, different, and enriching adventures in the journey of love.

You Can Love People You Don't Like

As we expand the circle of people that we have tender and loving feelings toward, we will also discover some or many people we don't feel at all attracted to. In fact, some people we know or meet arouse feelings of disgust, or dislike in us.

How do you handle relating to people that you just don't like—for whatever reason? Do you ignore them, gossip about them, shun them, or even act like you do like them?

There is yet another way to learn to love people you don't like. First of all you need to be aware of your real feelings. It is OK not to like someone. It is OK to feel repulsed by them. But the feeling itself should not be your last word on the relationship.

By acknowledging your feeling you can still learn to love that person. You do this by choosing to desire that person's fulfillment in life just as you desire that you and the people you really love become fulfilled.

In other words, even though you feel really irritable, frustrated, bored, or hostile toward someone, deep down you acknowledge your human kinship with them, and you wish them well in the journey of life. You may still feel repulsed by them, but at least you are not doing anything to bring harm or ill will to them. If you have never tried this approach in learning to love people who are unattractive, uninteresting, or repugnant to you, then I suggest that you practice it a few times to see if it might help you be more supportive and caring even to your enemies. As Jesus said, "Love your enemies...in order that you may be sons of your Father who is in heaven; for He causes His sun to rise on the evil and the good, and sends the rain on the righteous and the unrighteous" (Matt. 5:44,45).

We Need a Tougher Love

A healthy relationship, and one which we can experience with both our friends and our enemies, recognizes that honest conflict gives way to growth. Love doesn't mean not fighting. People who love each other and are close may need to fight occasionally. For friends, honest conflict can lead the way to feelings of respect and a new desire to negotiate and reach peaceful resolutions of differences.

A rule of thumb for knowing whether or not a particular feeling, value, or behavior is worth negotiating or even fighting about is as follows. If you have a negative feeling that persists for a long period of time in a relationship that you really care about, then you need to risk expressing that feeling.

Say, for instance, that in one of the friendships you are developing the other person does something that offends you, hurts you, or frustrates you. If the feeling of hurt or frustration persists for several hours or especially several days, then you need to tell your friend how you feel and what made you feel this way.

Such honest and open sharing of feelings clears the air of phoniness and gives your friend vital information about what values you have and what points of view you are taking. In turn, your friend can respond genuinely from his own unique set of values and feelings. In time, with sincere mutual efforts to communicate, you and your friend can come to new terms for how the friendship can grow deeper, and how you both may need to make concessions or changes in order to do so.

Continuous give-and-take is what keeps friendships alive, spontaneous, up to date, and mutually beneficial.

Conflict requires an attitude of faith—faith that your efforts will lead to the adequate resolution of the conflict. In creative conflict the struggles of honest disagreement give way to the emergence of an original solution. Even when we feel especially afraid that this may not happen, we must trust that God will in some original way bring His own wisdom and ingenuity to bear on the situation. Instead of selfishly clinging to our own point of view, we should remain humble enough to give and take until some new and perhaps surprising answer jumps into our awareness. The pathway to creative conflict and mutual growth will be both painful and joyful, both frightening and exciting. If we are truly seeking the best for our lives and relationships, we will not be put off by fear or pain along the way.

Love Allows for Uniqueness

The other side of openness and sharing, and just as important, is the respect for privacy that characterizes loving relationships. Love that does not allow another person to have solitude or some dimension of privacy becomes smothering and sticky. It is too possessive, too demanding to be part of someone's life all the time. Genuine love is more gentle than this. It knows how to "let go" and "let be." It is a more trusting love. To love someone in this way is to give them space to be themselves and support to grow in their own particular way. Vicki, one of my students, said it this way:

> Please don't confuse my aloneness with loneliness.
> I am not aloof or lonely, I am searching...
> Searching for that true self God has called me to be.
> My search may take me on a different path—
> an isolated one—but let me follow it.
> Don't drag me down your path. I am not
> equipped for its terrain.
> I must follow *my* path, even if it seems to lead
> me away from you.
> But don't worry. Even if our paths don't merge now,
> they will lead us to the same destination—
> unique selfhood in God.

This kind of commitment makes possible an emotional and spiritual bond that is dynamic and expansive, not static and constrictive, in nature. It opens the way for mutual enrichment through intellectual, emotional, and bodily levels of expression. There is a feeling of confidence in the relationship because there is a courage to discover each other at deeper and deeper levels, while still holding great respect for for each other's privacy.

Love Wants God's Will

As we focus our energies on becoming truly Christlike—able to love God, ourselves, and others as purely as He does—the Holy Spirit augments our natural efforts by gracing our lives with many gifts and talents for expressing love in the world.

This brings a deep inner harmony to our lives. Our

bodies, our emotions, and our values become unified in the operation of a "loving will." We become able to organize our entire being around the principle of *agape*—the love of God.

Of course all this doesn't happen overnight, any more than a plant or a baby can grow to full stature overnight. It is a lifetime process. Therefore, we must be patient with ourselves and others, whatever stage of growth we find. On the other hand, we need to be vigilant and alert as well, so that we do not miss the many opportunities for growth that God continually brings to our life. What we need are the paradoxical qualities of *relaxed alertness* and *gentle discipline* to make the best progress through life.

As we understand these things and surrender ourselves with trust to the Father's loving care, we can join the psalmist who declared: "I will bless the Lord who counsels me; he gives me wisdom in the night. He tells me what to do. I am always thinking of the Lord; and because he is near, I never need to stumble or to fall. Heart, body, and soul are filled with joy!" (Ps. 16:7-9, *TLB*).

An Exercise for Nurturing the Courage to Love

I wish to end this book with an exercise I believe will encourage you in the journey of love over a lifetime. Read through the entire exercise and then set aside a time and place for going through it on your own. It can be done once a day for several weeks. In fact, you can develop variations in the technique to fit your situation as time goes on. The technique itself is a guided fantasy which will help focus your inner energies in a way that facilitates your growth. The technique can readily be combined with prayer and meditation.

Find a quiet room and a comfortable chair, perhaps where you are sitting right now. Close your eyes and allow a few moments for bodily tensions and distracting thoughts to disappear. Let the mind become a blank screen.

Now begin to develop an image of yourself some months or years from this moment. Have faith to believe that by God's grace and your desire you have become a much more sensitive, wise, and loving person than you now are. It has been a slow and sometimes painful process, but now the fruit of growth is beginning to show. Vividly imagine yourself encountering in different scenes the people who are most important in your life. See what many ways you are now able to channel your love for them. Experiment in touching them verbally, emotionally, and physically. Discover what it is like to have a full, loving encounter. See what kinds of ways love has taught you to serve them and make their lives richer.

Now move your attention from this core network of intimate loved ones to a more peripheral network of friends and acquaintances. How might you express your love to your neighbors, your boss or employees, your relatives, or your colleagues. Watch yourself as you go about loving each one and adding something special to his or her life. Notice the kind of atmosphere your love creates wherever you go. You might even picture yourself handling anger, irritation, or conflict in a gracious but direct way. Your firm love enables you to be honest, sensitive, and direct—even in expressing your disagreements. Your love is still able to flow into people's lives.

Now let your awareness turn to humanity. The countless individuals whom you will never meet, but who are desperately in need of love. Let a few nameless faces appear before you. Let your heart go out to them. Let your heart be touched by their need and suffering, even though there is nothing specifically you can do other than being profoundly aware of them.

And, last, let your awareness turn to God. Meditate on the words of Jesus: "By this all men will know that you are My disciples, if you have love for one another" (John 13:35).

Let gratitude sweep through your being for the journey of

love that God is enabling you to follow. Warmly embrace Jesus who has faithfully revealed His own loving heart to you, and who has graciously made His life yours, and your life His. Look into His eyes and see if He has something to say to you. Spend a few moments with Him, and then prepare to come back to the present moment—sitting in your chair where you began.

Now come back to full awareness of this present moment. In this process you have been able to give yourself something real and precious. You have given yourself a glimpse of the real transformation that is occurring in the depths of your being. You have given your body, your feelings, and your thoughts a vivid symbol around which they can organize the psychological and spiritual energies of your life. But remember that the growth process itself is slow and gradual.

You are beginning to know what it is to be fully youself and deeply Christlike. You are learning what it means to live out of the divine core of your personality—channeling and harnessing your life energies in the service of God's loving will. And this is the courage to love.

An important aspect of my growth as an author is feedback I receive from you, the reader. I am interested in knowing what happens when you apply principles in the book to your life. You may give me personal feedback by writing in care of REGAL BOOKS, P.O. Box 1591, Glendale, Ca., 91209.

Notes

1. Morton Kelsey, *The Other Side of Silence* (New York: Paulist Press, 1976), pp.17,19.

2. Adrian Van Kaam, *The Woman at the Well* (Denville, NJ: Dimension Books, 1976), p. 57.

3. Rollo May, *Love and Will* (New York: W.W. Norton and Company, 1969), p. 133.

4. Billy Graham, *How to Be Born Again* (Waco, TX: Word Books, 1977).

5. Sidney Jourard, *The Transparent Self: Self Disclosure and Well-Being* (New York: D. Van Nostrand Company, 1964), p. 21.

6. Morton Kelsey, *The Other Side of Silence* (New York: Paulist Press, 1976), p. 111.

7. Adrian Van Kaam, *Looking for Jesus* (Denville, NJ: Dimension Books, 1978), p. 92.

8. By permission of Jules Feiffer. © Copyright 1974 Field Enterprises, Inc. Courtesy of Field Newspaper Syndicate.

9. Alexander Lowen, *The Way to Vibrant Health* (New York: Harper and Row Publishers, 1977).

10. Rollo May, *The Art of Counseling* (Nashville: Abingdon Press, 1967), p. 177.

11. Everett Shostrum, *Actualizing Therapy: Foundations for a Scientific Ethic* (San Diego: EDITS, 1976).

12. Everett L. Shostrum and Dan Montgomery, *Healing Love: How God Works Within the Personality* (Nashville, TN: Abingdon Press, 1978).

13. Fritz Kunkel, *In Search of Maturity* (New York: Charles Scribner's Sons, 1946), p. 254.

14. Kahlil Gibran, *The Prophet* (New York: Alfred A. Knopf, 1923), pp. 11,12.

15. Keith Miller, *Please Love Me* (Waco, TX: Word Books, 1977), p. 66.